IN THE PALM OF HIS HAND

A Devotional Journey
Written by Teens for Teens

Terry K. Dittmer, Editor

D1374049

Unless otherwise noted, the Scripture quotations in this publication are from The Holy Bible: NEW INTERNATIONAL VERSION, © 1973, 1978, 1984 by the International Bible Society. Used by permission of Zondervan Bible Publishers.

Copyright © 1988 Concordia Publishing House
3558 S. Jefferson Avenue, St. Louis, MO 63118-3968
Manufactured in the United States of America

1 2 3 4 5 6 7 8 9 10   97 96 95 94 93 92 91 90 89 88

Contents

Foreword

In the Palm of His Hand is the perfect title for this devotional book. For that is how the writers of this book stand with their Savior, and that is the Lord's relationship with you as well.

This devotional journey is the work of 18 select young people and 8 adults. These 26 persons gathered together for a week of study and learning in June 1987. The Young Writer's Workshop they participated in was sponsored by the Board for Youth Services, Aid Association for Lutherans of Appleton, WI, and Concordia Publishing House.

The result was devotions, written for youth by youth and a few youthful adults, which have now found their way into your palms.

These pages have been tested and approved by young people throughout the country. They have been written and rewritten in keeping with the spontaneity and freshness of ideas that are relevant to youthful readers.

I'm excited about this book! It deals with the real, live issues and concerns of real, live young people. If it is true (and I believe it is) that young people can minister very effectively to each other, then this book will be useful to anyone dealing with the problems and challenges of contemporary coming of age.

Life's journey can be very frustrating. One of the authors calls life "a desert filled with problems too hot to be solved." Another runs "the marathon of life." Still another walks through a black forest where "I grope along in the darkness and stumble on the broken dreams that lie strewn across the path."

Yet, I am most impressed that the message of hope keeps popping up throughout these pages. "You will continue the good work You started in me." "Help me to accept other people as

You have accepted me for Jesus' sake." "God is with me every step of the way, and He will direct the steps I take."

These devotions come out of actual experiences of young people who comfortingly emphasize in many different ways that all of us, youth and adults alike, are "in the palm of His hand."

The developers of this book pray that you will find these pages very practical and meaningful. As this book helps encourage you to continue to develop your devotional life, you can use it in many ways:

1. Read a devotion each morning or evening for the next 102 days.
2. Take the book with you to school or work and open it when you have a free moment.
3. Use it in family devotions.
4. Share it with your friends at appropriate times.
5. Keep it handy in your room so that you can use it to share your faith with others and stay connected with God's love yourself.
6. Give it to a friend who you think could be helped by it.

Along with the other authors I pray that our efforts will enrich your personal prayer life. This book may even inspire you to write devotions and prayers of your own. And that's great also! If you do and if you want to share them with us, please do so. Perhaps we can have In the Palm of His Hand, Book II coming out soon!

Blessings to you as you see the Lord at work in your daily life, connecting your faith with all your experiences. Have a hopefilled journey as your devotional life is strengthened and as you continue to walk in the palm of God's hand.

RICH BIMLER
Executive Secretary, Board for Youth Services
The Lutheran Church—Missouri Synod

9

The Relativity of the Law of Sines
Jer. 29:11

Fifth hour. Trigonometry.

I'm struggling to stay awake as I stare at some angles. The teacher's voice pierces my fog as she explains the law of sines.

Suddenly it hits me. Who cares? I mean, will it ever matter that I know that the sine of *angle A* over *side a* equals the sine of *angle B* over *side b* equals the sine of *angle C* over *side c*? Five years from now will this mean anything to me? Will I even remember it?

Sometimes my whole life seems like that. I struggle along and suddenly think, "Who cares? Will my life make any difference in this world? Will anyone even remember me . . . care what I'm doing or where I'm going?"

I don't know the equation. But God does. At least He says He does, and I believe it. That's part of faith, and I guess that's what matters. Whatever I do, whatever I say, whatever I become, God gives me hope for the future. Because He bought me with Christ's blood, He will also use me to accomplish His good will. That matters.

Prayer: Thanks for Your promises, Lord. Sometimes I'm afraid that I'm a totally useless person. Thank You for promising to use me to do Your work. Give me peace as I remember that You have a plan for me in Christ. Amen.

A. S.

Accepted Rom. 15:7–9

I usually look forward to baby-sitting, but I felt unsure the other night. I hadn't met the child.

I shouldn't have worried. As I walked through the door, the face of the 3-year-old lit up, and her chubby arms immediately encircled my legs. As she dragged me away, anxious to show me her bedroom, her mother explained, "Stacy's been very excited about your coming."

What a great feeling—to be accepted by someone before she even knows me! It wouldn't have mattered to Stacy if I were short or tall, fat or thin, beautiful or not-so-beautiful. She didn't care how smart I was, or how athletic, or what neighborhood I lived in. Stacy accepted me just because I was her baby-sitter.

That happens at my church too. I have some really great friends there. They don't care what I look like or how I act. They just accept me as another one of God's children.

We are that way at our church because that's how God is. It doesn't matter whether I eat with knife and fork, or even whether I go to church every Sunday.

God accepts me because Christ's death and resurrection cleared my name. I have His forgiveness, and that's it. I am accepted!

Prayer: Thanks for Your acceptance, Lord. I know I often fall short and don't deserve it. But I know You always forgive me and give me another chance. Help me to accept other people as You have accepted me for Jesus' sake. Amen.

A. S.

Losses to Gain   Joshua 1:9

I struggled to wake up this morning. Today is a day I don't want to go through. Today I leave behind many of the things I love— friends, school, church. My family is moving. Again!

I feel empty. I am past disbelief, past anger, past fear. My emotions have gone on strike.

* * * * *

That day happened two years ago, but I still hurt. I still miss my friends. Sometimes I wish I could go back in time.

Oh, I don't totally regret the move. Since then, I've met new friends, adjusted to my new school, and grown to love my new church. But more than that, God has taught me.

He's taught me about trust. When there are no familiar faces around, God is the only one I can trust. When I'm not in control, He is.

He's taught me about love—His love for me. He's listened to my angry cries in the night, and He has comforted me to sleep.

God has taught me about life too. I know that problems and struggles will always face me, but somehow God is using—and will use—all the trash I live through to make me a stronger person. He has promised that He will be with me wherever I go.

Prayer: Life's tough, God. I get mad, and I question You a lot. I know inside that You're in control. Help me to see a reason for all this pain. In Jesus I pray. Amen.

A. S.

We Are His Workmanship

Eph. 2:10

I discovered in my dictionary that one synonym for "workmanship" is *art*. That opened a new understanding of Eph. 2:10. We are the artwork of God!

Artists use their work to say something to their audience. What does God want me, His artwork, to say to the world? Three things to start with:

Glorify God. Christ was the ultimate expression of God's glory. Nothing could be more glorious than Jesus' resurrection. We too are made to express the glory of God. "Whether you eat or drink or whatever you do, do it all for the glory of God" (1 Cor. 10:31).

Love Others. Jesus, the ultimate expression of love, died a painful death carrying the sins of all generations. Out of sight! Since He did that for all people as well as for me, I strive to share that same love with others.

Serve Others. Christ was the ultimate expression of service—not only in death but in life. The night of the Last Supper Jesus bent down to wash the feet of His disciples. Since the Son of God was willing to serve mortals, shouldn't I also be willing to do so?

These are generalities. What are our specific "good works" to be to share His message with the world? Look around. "God prepared [them] in advance for us to do."

Prayer: Help me fulfill my potential as an expression of Your love, Lord. Work in and through me today to serve others, that I may serve You and so glorify You through Your Son Jesus. Amen.

A. S.

My Father Said He Loved Me

Ps. 127

Last night my dad finally said he loved me. I wonder why it's so hard for him.

It was a rather ordinary evening. We were just sitting at the kitchen table, Dad paying some bills, and I working on some homework. We weren't really saying much of anything to each other.

Most of the time when we do talk it's the regular teen-parent kind of stuff. You know. Dad says, "I don't want you doing that." Or he says, "I'd better not catch you doing such and such." Or, "Back when I was you age, blah, blah, blah." And I mostly just say "yeah" or grunt something back.

It's not that we don't like each other. My dad's okay, all things considered. And I think he basically respects my space. We just don't talk about it much.

So it was kind of weird last night. He and I, sitting there, kind of aware of each other. Suddenly he just up and says, "I love you, Son." It was amazing, Lord. It really was. It felt so good to hear him say it. It felt so good to hear the words. It was really wonderful.

And then I did something I don't do very often. I said, "I love you too, Dad," Last night makes me wonder though. If it feels so good to hear it, why don't we say it more often?

Prayer: Thank You for Your love, and thank You for my father. Help me to love him and not be so stingy in showing it. In Jesus' name. Amen.

T. D.

Did You?

Do you? It's Friday morning at school and everybody wants to know if you have a date for the weekend. And they want to know with whom . . . unless you're going steady, of course. Then they already know.

It's Monday morning and the question changes tense and takes on new implications. "Did you?" now means, "Did you have sex?"

It seems like everybody thinks that to have a good time you have to have sex. It's like guys and girls can't just have fun together and enjoy each other's company. You have to get physical.

Why can't guys and girls just be friends? Why can't we just talk, or go out for pizza, or go to a movie, or listen to music—just because we're friends? Why is there always such pressure to go farther?

Why is there even such pressure to date? Why can't a group of guys and girls go out together . . . as friends?

Jesus enjoyed the company of men and women. Why can't teens?

Prayer: Lord, thank You for friends. Thank You for the time we can spend together talking, laughing, playing, enjoying each other. Help me to be a friend to the people You've given to me. Amen.

T. D.

What's Right and What's Wrong?

Ps. 112

Marcy's mother tells her all about contraception so Marcy will be protected "because everybody knows that all teens are doing *it*," and her mother doesn't want Marcy to get caught.

Jim's parents open their liquor cabinet to him and his friends because, they say, "All teens are drinking, and we would rather have you drink at home than out on the streets where somebody might get hurt."

Bob's parents rent X-rated videos to show on their home VCR. Bob's not supposed to see the films, but his parents don't do a whole lot to keep him or his friends from sneaking a peek.

Shelly's parents have always made a big deal about her going to Sunday school every single week, as though she's personally going to meet the devil if she doesn't. Shelly asks, "Why don't they think they should be in Bible class too? Isn't the devil just as interested in them?"

Sometimes it's hard to tell what's right and what's wrong, especially when parents or other adults send mixed signals. Sometimes adults are inconsistent!

I'm glad God has shared His outline for living in His Word. I'm glad His guidelines are forever and never change. I'm glad I can trust God's way to be perfect and keep me safe.

Prayer: Lord, preserve me in Your way. Help me to know the difference between right and wrong, and forgive me when I make a mistake, for Jesus' sake. Amen.

T. D.

I've Got the Spirit   Acts 2:37–47

This morning church was so dead! The singing was sad. The people there seemed to be bored. The organ was dreary. And the pastor seemed to preach forever. I heard some people say it was a very good sermon, but I couldn't find my way through it.

I sometimes think about Pentecost. I remember that the Bible says the disciples were excited. The Holy Spirit came to them, and they couldn't contain their enthusiasm for Jesus Christ. They preached to people they didn't know in languages they didn't know they could speak. They were enthusiastic . . . excited . . . fired up.

Sometimes I think church services should be like a pep rally before a football game. Like, there we are, excited about the home team, God's team.

I once met a lady who said she was filled with the Spirit. She loved God. She loved people. She loved her church. She sang songs of praise with joy like I've never heard before. She prayed with a fervor, as though she really believed her prayers would be answered. She cared about people and went out of her way to lend a helping hand. She wasn't weird, and she didn't do some of those strange things—like speaking in tongues, or healing, or laying on hands, or things like that. She just said she loved her Lord. And if that's what it means to be Spirit-filled, I like the idea.

Prayer: O Lord, fill me with Your Spirit so that I live for You, celebrating that You have made me a part of Your family, and doing all things with joy and enthusiasm, for Jesus' sake. Amen.

T. D.

18

The Last Game   Gal. 1:10

It's all over. Victory was so close we could almost hold it in our sweaty palms. Then it was gone. We lost it. *I* lost it. I made a mistake, and the whole team fell apart. Our eyes called to the coach for help, but there was nothing he could do.

The last game is now a tearful memory, and each player feels alone in the loss. But the coach calls gently, "Come here; I still love you." Strange words to be spoken, but so good to hear.

All of a sudden, I understand something new. I don't have to worry about earning love or acceptance; it's already there. Coach can't give us victory, but he can help tie us together. We may be defeated, but we are still a team. I no longer feel afraid.

No matter that I lose, no matter how hard the team may fall, there is One who is here forever. He gives us gifts to be used to their fullest, yet the trophies and prizes of this world mean nothing to Him. Not even losing the biggest game can change His love for us in Jesus Christ. He'll never break His promises, and He'll never stop His wonderful love.

The sports season may be over for now, but our life in victory is just beginning.

Prayer: Dear God, thank You for all Your gifts to me. Forgive me when I fail to use them to my best ability. Thank You for never seeing me as a loser. Please keep me in the hope that all who set their sights on You never really lose. Amen.

K. L. D.

Who You Callin' Too Young?

1 Tim. 4:12

"No!" the pastor said firmly. "It would be too difficult for her to be an acolyte."

"Why?" demanded Joanie in the midst of her sixth-grade Sunday school class.

The pastor continued in fatherly fashion, "You, I, and even her mom can see that a blind girl would have trouble lighting the candles."

"Well, I'll help her," insisted Joanie. "She's my friend, and it'll work. Wait and see!"

The pastor, surprised at Joanie's boldness, agreed, with great reservations, to let the girls try it. So he, along with the entire congregation, was delighted and inspired that first Sunday when the two girls lit the altar candles together. Their determination had paid off.

It took a lot of guts for Joanie to do what she did. Even though she held no title, she was, in every sense of the word, a leader. She was following St. Paul's advice, "Don't let anyone look down on you because you are young, but set an example for the believers in speech, in life, in love, in faith and in purity."

Prayer: Dear God, help me see the endless opportunities You provide for me to be a leader. Give me courage to take a stand and, in the process, to set an example for others. Sometimes it will be tough, but remind me that You're always there leading me so that I can lead others to You. Amen.

K. L. D.

Those Special Friends   Gal. 6:2

I've always been a talker. My parents say that I was born giving orders to the doctor and I haven't shut up since.

Talking is an important part of communication. However, far too often we overlook something equally important: listening.

I am no exception. I used to talk and talk to a friend of mine, never realizing that he seldom spoke a word. But one day our conversation took a different path. My friend felt really low. He needed to talk to someone, and he chose me.

That's when I learned how to listen and keep my mouth shut. For once, I didn't stop myself from letting Jesus help me be like Him. It felt strange at first, but as the conversation progressed, I began to realize the joy that can come from listening. Just saying "I understand" to someone I cared about felt wonderful—especially since I already had discovered how good it feels to be listened to and understood.

God has provided us with a great source of support and love through His gift of fellowship in Jesus Christ. With His help, we are able to share our experiences, give advice, or just listen with care to those around us. To have someone to share with is a most precious thing. But to be a person with whom others can talk, to be trusted, is a gift of God.

Prayer: Dear God, Thank You so much for giving me people with whom I can talk. Help me also use your gift of Christian fellowship to be an understanding, caring, and willing listener. Amen.

K. L. D.

The Burden of Failure   Phil. 4:13

"Why aren't you running for secretary?" Craig asked surprised. "You're a neat person, and you've got student council experience. You'd do great. Hey—I'd vote for you!"

"Thanks, but I just can't make myself do it," Brenda replied.

"Why not?"

"Well, what if I lost?" Brenda moaned. "I'd look like a fool. I just can't take the risk."

Many of us have faced similar situations. I know I have. I used to allow my fear of failure to haunt me so badly that I wouldn't try anything unless I was sure I wouldn't fail.

Then a friend said, "Think about the possibility of success rather than failure. After all, God made each of us good at something. If we will remember His strength and His desire to carry our fears for us, then we can gather up the courage to keep trying new things."

That encouragement changed my outlook on life and made me a happier person. Sure, I still experience failure. But I've found new joy in knowing that I tried. And the best joy comes from knowing that, in failure or success, Jesus loves me and stands by me.

Prayer: Dear God, many times I get frustrated with myself because I want to succeed too much. Help me realize that I won't always fail, that You have given me talents to achieve, and that You love me no matter what. Help me keep on trying to find and use Your talents in me. Amen.

K. L. D.

But I Know He's Wrong

Dear Lord,

I got mad at one of my teachers today. He said some things that bothered me, things that I know are wrong. He voiced opinions that go against Your teachings. No, I didn't say anything to him out loud, but inside I was really angry. I felt like shouting. I wanted to tell him off right then and there. But I knew You wouldn't have liked that.

Lord, it's really hard to be patient. It seems like everything he says makes You look bad. Sometimes it's really hard to keep from showing my anger.

Please give me patience with this man, dear Jesus, and give me love. I pray that You would forgive him for the many times he has shortchanged You. And forgive me also, Lord, for the hostile feelings I have had towards him. Give me a chance to show this man Your love and grace. Give me a chance to show him what he's been missing.

In Your name. Amen.

A. H.

Brick after Brick

Ps. 144:15

Have you ever had the feeling that you were lugging around a load of bricks? A burden that was just too much to bear? I've had that feeling many times. Some people call it depression.

Maybe your Algebra grade just dropped again. Or maybe you're tired of listening to your parents constantly argue. Or maybe, no matter how hard you try, you just can't seem to make the team.

You're probably not desperate enough to go to a psychologist, but that load of bricks gets heavier every day.

Well, there is good news for you. You have your own personal counselor who will gladly help you with your load. He doesn't charge $70 an hour. He is available 24 hours a day. And He loves you more than anyone does. I'm talking about Jesus Christ.

The psalmist writes, "Blessed are the people whose God is the Lord." How right he is! God promises that He loves us and will never, ever forsake us. He cares for us so much that He wants us to come to Him daily with all our cares and concerns. When we cast our troubles on Him we are truly blessed, for our God is the Lord, and with Him nothing is impossible.

Prayer: Heavenly Father, You invite us to come to You with all our troubles—and right now, I have some burdens that are just too much for me to bear. Please remove this load of bricks from me, Lord, that I may be better able to serve You. Thank You, Jesus, for Your everlasting grace and love. Amen.

A. H.

Of Burger Flipping and Floor Mopping

Eph. 6:7

I worked at the local burger joint all summer, and, let me tell you, I hated it! Standing over a hot grill flipping greasy slabs of soybean for seven straight hours is not exactly my idea of fun. None of the other jobs at the place was all that intellectually stimulating either—making drinks, clearing tables, and sweeping floors. I guess someone had to do it, but why me? To make matters worse, I was always at odds with my boss and the rest of the employees.

One day while complaining to one of my buddies about the hot, messy job I had, I stopped thinking about myself and began to look around me. I saw friends who had lower-paying jobs than I had. Some worked under conditions that even I would have rejected. Still other friends had no jobs at all. Finally I realized that the Lord had really blessed me.

From then on I viewed my job in a whole different light. I began to see the benefits of it and looked for the good traits in my fellow workers. I began to thank God that He had given me this chance to earn some money and serve other people.

I realize now what a blessing the Lord gave me in such a seemingly lowly task, and I thank Him for it.

Prayer: Dear Lord, I don't always realize what Your blessings are, and I'm sorry for the times I complain when I should rejoice. Please forgive me. Thank You, Jesus, for all Your unrecognized blessings. Amen.

A. H.

What? Youth Group Fun?

Matt. 18:20

I'm always surprised when I hear other kids make remarks like, "Youth group; oh, how boring" or, "All we ever do is study the Bible." It makes me stop and wonder why our youth group is so great. Those remarks also help me thank the Lord for being part of such a great group.

Are you one of those people who think youth group is boring? If so, I assure you from experience that it is possible to have a great time and still be praising the Lord. Yes! At the same time!

Perhaps what has worked for our youth group will work for yours. It's worth a try.

We mix fun and worship. In other words, in anything we do, we praise God. Sure we study the Bible, but we do other things as well—play games, go to the movies, go on retreats. I believe God helps us enjoy ourselves more when we are gathered in His name. Even when we goof around, we are reminders to each other that God is with us, helping us have a good time. Then, when we have Bible study or worship, we can praise the Lord for all He has done for us.

God's great! The group's great! My friends are great!

Prayer: Dear Lord, thank You for all my friends, especially those who believe in You. Please bless the time that we're gathered in Your Name, and bring Your Holy Spirit down upon us to give us that extra joy that only You can give. Thank You, Jesus. Amen.

A. H.

What Should I Do? 1 Cor. 10:13

Lord,

What should I do? Why can't someone give me some answers?

The simple decisions, like picking out which socks to wear or whether or not to do an English assignment, come easily enough. But lately I've been told I need to do things that will affect the rest of my life.

My friends wonder why I am still sober and have not done *it* yet. They don't understand my confusion in following a set of morals that the world forgot about long ago. And, frankly, Lord, sometimes I forget too.

I want to be considered normal, so, why don't I go out and get drunk every weekend? Why don't I do *it* with just anyone? Lord, I know I'm not an angel, but it seems I have to commit a huge sin to be considered human in the eyes of the world.

Please help me resist temptation. Keep me strong and make Your will for me my will too. Amen.

J. B.

It Happened
James 5:19–20

It happened. I knew it would. Was there something I could have done? Could I have helped him?

My friend died last night. A car wreck—at least that's what my mom tried to tell me. But I knew better.

My friend had been sick, very sick, for a long time. It was an illness that I had watched and felt helpless to stop.

Alcohol had become a crutch for an otherwise lovable, kind, funny person. The more he drank, the more he swore he wasn't addicted. And then it happened.

Was there something I could have done? I talked, explained, argued, and debated—but that only made him more stubborn. Eventually I stopped talking because he stopped listening. I was afraid if I pushed too hard he would hate me.

I sometimes even wondered if it was all that wrong anyway. After all, he wasn't hurting anyone else—right? Wrong. I watched his mother at the funeral today. She was devastated. I could see that my friend had hurt a lot of other people too.

I remember he had always said that nothing would happen to him, that he'd be alright. But he wasn't. He isn't alright at all any more.

Prayer: Help me, Lord, be a better friend and a comfort to my friends who are struggling with an addiction. Give me the courage, even when they won't listen to reason, to be a witness of Your concern even in their struggle. Help us together to find healing in Your caring love. For Jesus' sake. Amen.

J. B.

Thomas and Us   John 20:24–29

Thomas! What a lack of faith he had! How unreasonable he was! He wouldn't believe when the other disciples told him that they had seen the Lord.

Thomas said, "Unless I see the nail marks in his hands and put my finger where the nails were, and put my hand into his side, I will not believe it."

We are outraged that Thomas wouldn't believe. But aren't we all like doubting Thomas at one time or another?

Doubting is a part of human nature, and Thomas was human just as we are. Still, we put him down for his lack of faith in the Lord's promise that He would rise on the third day.

The Lord understood Thomas' need, and He revealed Himself to him, and Thomas' faith was strengthened.

Today the Holy Spirit continues to reveal Jesus to us through the Scriptures. One of the best ways to *see* Jesus is to read God's Word letting the Holy Spirit guide us.

Jesus' promises are true for today—for everyday—especially the promise of His forgiveness for our own doubts.

Prayer: O Lord, when we're filled with doubt, open our hearts to the truth of Your love and forgiveness. Fill us with Your Spirit so that we may always celebrate You as our living Savior. Amen.

J. B.

31

I'll Never Speak to Her Again!

Matt. 18:21–22

Have you ever held a grudge? I have. Grudges seem to be a part of life. Jack gets mad at Jill for what she said to him, how she looked at him, or what she told his best friend about him. Suddenly he is holding a grudge. If you've ever held a grudge, you know it isn't easy. We grudge-holders must at all costs avoid any *civil* conversation with that person. We can't be seen with her friends; and whenever there's a gossip session, we've got to throw in a list of her latest crimes. After a while this list gets harder to maintain, but we keep telling ourselves we've got to keep it up.

For all this hard work we only hurt ourselves. We tend to be easily irritated and unhappy because of the bitterness inside. Keeping up with the gossip gets complicated, and messing up a story can mean losing even more friends. We usually end up with less than what we started with.

So how do we get around the old grudge? One word: forgiveness. Thank the Lord, God didn't hold a grudge against us. If He had, we would all be doomed to hell. But He didn't do that. He forgave us. One of the best ways we can thank Him for that is to forgive others when they sin against us.

Prayer: O Lord, forgive me for the grudges and grievances I bear. Where my relationship with another is strained or broken, guide me to reconciliation. Help us forgive each other, for Jesus' sake. Amen.

J. B.

Me Care for *Them*? Gal. 6:1

"Did you hear? Tammy got VD. Probably from Chuck."

"Gross! Who all knows?"

"My mom told me, so I guess the whole world knows by now."

"Oh, great! Well, there go two more friends. I can't risk catching anything from them. AIDS, you know. It's real!"

"Yeah, I know. Besides, my dad won't let me hang out with kids who mess around. He's afraid I'll try it. If I ever got pregnant or got VD, I couldn't go home again."

How can we help Tammy and Chuck? St. Paul encourages us to care about and for those caught in sin. At the same time he cautions us not to be tempted to the same sin.

You know that Jesus deals with you and your private sins the same way He dealt with the woman caught in adultery—with patience, love, kindness, forgiveness, and gentleness (John 8:3–11). That's the way He wants to deal with all Tammys and Chucks. He does that through His Word and sacraments. And He also uses you to act out His love.

You, better than anyone, know your Tammy and Chuck. And you, better than anyone, can speak God's forgiving words of restoration in a way that Tammy and Chuck will understand.

Prayer: Dear Jesus, when the time comes, give me courage to talk with my friends. Let Your Holy Spirit help me choose the right words of Your forgiveness and love. Amen.

M. A. M.

Taking Time Out with Jesus

Ps. 119:105

"Watcha doin', Little One?"

Brenda recognized the voice: Paula—captain of every girl's team in school, straight A's, brassy. Brenda sat up, furtively closing her Bible and turning it upside down on the ground.

"You read that book often?"

"Yeah," Brenda replied, "I try to. Or at least to do some thinking and praying about a passage I know."

"How come? It only makes you feel guilty. I mean, who can understand it anyway? I decided long ago just to be the best person I can. God can't expect more of me than that."

"I like being close to God," Brenda said softly, eyes on the ground, "Last year, when my cousin Erik died of leukemia, he thanked Jesus for being with him, for forgiving him, and for helping him face his trip to heaven."

"That's simply too sweet for words."

Ignoring the comment Brenda continued, "If God's Word could do that for Erik when he was dying, I wanted to find out what it could do for me when I wasn't. Paula, maybe you don't have problems; you're good at everything. But me . . . well, let's just say that God really has to help me get through the day."

Paula hesitated, looked around, then sat down next to Brenda and asked, "But, what do you *say* to God?"

Prayer: Dear Jesus, sometimes I'm Brenda, sometimes Paula. As I meditate on Your Word, help me apply to myself the Good News that You love me, forgive me, and are with me always. Amen.

M. A. M.

Every Day's an Easter   1 Peter 1:3–9

"That's disgusting," I told my uncle. He, who was slowly dying of cancer, was wondering whether to invest in expensive shoes or buy cheap ones year by year.

He had been weird for a long time. Once when we all went swimming, he stepped on a broken bottle and, cut through to the bone, never swore once. Just swam ashore, had my dad carry him across the sand to the car, and went for stitches. And when he left for home he laughed about how ridiculous he looked on crutches.

When my brother died and my mom swore at God, he just told her that God understood her anger and still loved her. Even when Grandpa died, my uncle just hummed Easter hymns and did what was necessary for the funeral.

So when he told us about his shoe problem I yelled, "Don't you realize how serious this is?"

"Sure," he said calmly, "life is serious, and we may all have to endure trials we don't understand. So what? The war between God and evil is over. And God won!"

"So?"

"So, we can rejoice in our faith and the ultimate salvation that comes from it." And he started humming Easter hymns again.

Prayer: Dear heavenly Father, so many things worry me, scare me, hurt me. The Easter hymn says, "Jesus lives, the victory's won." Help me have so much faith and confidence in Your Son that I can say with Peter, I am shielded by Your power, even while suffering trials. Amen.

M. A. M.

Praise the Lord Ps. 148

O strange and wondrous world by God the wondrous made:
Surprises freely hurled around! A grand parade!
Outlandish ostrich, preening peacock: winged throng
Of feathered rainbows, effervescent heavenly song;
Befuddled puppies tripping kittens swatting air;
And fledglings, ears acock for insects unaware:
Oh, praise the Lord!

Upthrusting mountains, stretching plains and placid rills
'Neath river clouds soon dammed to cleanse from vaulted sills;
Cascading sun rays, orange from distant dust and storm,
A stage for nature's inborn song, a chorus formed;
Magnolias, orchids, lilacs—frail petals hued;
Abundant fields, distended silos, fruit imbued;
Oh, praise the Lord!

Creation's crown, God's image filled by Spirit breath,
Divinely molded, born anew, the seed of Seth:
Minutely sculptured baby fingers grasping mine,
Encircling freedom, hope, adulthood, age's lines.
O strange and wondrous world by God the wondrous made;
Surprises freely hurled around! A grand parade!
Oh, praise the Lord!

M. A. M.

More than Raiding the Clothes Closet
Prov. 11:16

My sister's clothes closet has always been a challenge for me. Over the years of my borrowing things from her closet in the morning, my sister has developed some incredible security methods. Not only do her bedroom and closet doors squeak loudly enough to be heard over the noise of the blow dryer and coffee pot, but she has some hidden arrangement of clothing so that she knows exactly what has been touched when she goes back to check later in the morning. Regardless of how frustrated I get, I love sneaking into her room in the morning if only for the attention I get.

My sister is a whole lot more than a person to borrow clothes from. She was there when I, at age two, fell down the cement steps and scraped my knee. She was there as I, at age five, stepped onto the big yellow school bus for the first time. She was there at age eight to send me off to camp. She was there when I, at age eleven, discovered the opposite sex for the very first time. She's here now to talk to whenever I need her.

Prayer: Lord, thank You for my sister. I know I haven't always appreciated her. Instead, I think about myself and everything I need. Teach me to love her at all times—even when her new boyfriend or part-time job seems a lot more important than I am. Be with both of us so that we can grow up together in Your love. Amen.

B. F.

Yuck Days

Luke 5:1–7

Yuck Days—everyone has them. Whether it's a Monday morning after a wild, sleepless weekend or a Friday afternoon that seems to go on forever, bad times happen right at the moment you need them the least.

On a hot summer day, your double-scoop ice cream cone suddenly begins to melt, and huge globs of slimy goop fall to the dirty pavement. A test with a red *F* on the top is returned. An endless list of "to do's" is left for you on the kitchen table. Your boss schedules you to work the Saturday of the beach party. Whatever the trouble may be, it seems like a huge roadblock to you at that time in your life.

Even Peter had a yuck day. He had been out on a musty, smelly lake at night, no icy Coke to keep him going, and no bug spray. He was counting on a good catch to bring in a little cash for the next week, but, you guessed it: no fish. A definite yuck day!

Then, without drum roll or fanfare, Jesus appeared and suggested he try again. You can just imagine Peter's reaction: "You gotta be joking! I've been out there all night on the lake and no fish."

Well, Peter tried the suggestion anyway. He put the net out, and the fish came in. The Lord was there for him. He turned Peter's yuck day into a hooray day!

Prayer: Lord, help my yuck days become hooray days. Develop my attitude so that I'm not easily put down or frustrated. Help me see Your great blessings in everything around me. Please be there. Amen.

B. F.

A Root Beer with Two Straws

Ps. 34:8–9

A friend once defined happiness as a root beer with two straws. She meant happiness was both enjoying something great and having a friend to enjoy it with. I like to enjoy my root beer, but I often feel that there's no one to enjoy it with.

Like at school. The days can be pretty depressing. Seems like most kids just stare into space, totally disinterested. They're not happy. They won't share their root beers.

Or like at parties. Everyone looks like they're having a good time. But some parties are like an epidemic of false faces, contests to see who can fake the best time. Everybody has taken hours to get ready, each in designer clothes, out to impress . . . but not really happy.

I think I've learned that I can't count on putting my straw into someone else's root beer. I need to find my own. And I have. Having the Lord inside me makes me happy. And that's worth inviting others to dip their straws into.

Prayer: Lord, help me to think of You as a bottomless glass of cold, refreshing, delicious root beer. Always keep my straw in You and make me willing to let others put in their straws to taste and see that the Lord is good. Help us be truly happy together. Amen.

B. F.

Twenty-Four Hour Toll-Free Number

Luke 15:11–24

After a late practice at school, I left the building without thinking, slamming the door behind me. But I needed a ride home, the school door was locked, and I was uptown without a quarter to call home. At that moment, I could only talk to my Dad in heaven.

The knowledge of my heavenly Father's openness is a real comfort. He is there 24 hours a day, ready to listen at absolutely no cost. That's not always true between earthly dads and children. Misunderstandings, lack of time, and not having a quarter can block effective human communication.

Like the prodigal son, I often stray from God when things are okay. I think, "Why do I need God when I'm having a great time without Him?" The unavoidable crash soon comes, though, and the party is over. Then I run back to the Lord, asking for forgiveness and looking for some kind of hope.

The welcome I get is superhuman. That's the point. The Lord isn't human. He's God. And because He is, I am free to "pray continually" to Him (1 Thess. 5:17). He's there when I'm in trouble or feeling lonely. He's there when I'm feeling happy and ready to praise. He's even there if I just want to say hi.

Prayer: Yes, Lord, now is one of those times. I need You in my life and I ask You to listen. Don't let me forget Your love and blessings. Thank You for being my 24-hour toll free number. Amen.

B. F.

Grandparents Are . . . ? Lev. 19:32

My friend Leigh's grandmother just came to live with her. Leigh hates it! She says her grandmother is weird—always talking about things nobody else cares about, always interfering and messing up life at home. Leigh wishes her grandmother had never come to live with them.

I don't understand Leigh. My grandparents are gone—to heaven. But, oh, how I miss them! My grandpa used to live with us. It wasn't always easy for my mom, but I thought Grandpa was neat!

And my grandma . . . . I still remember the week she died. On Wednesday I had my hair cut and asked my mother if we could show it to Grandma right away. Mom said she'd see it on Sunday. But that Sunday with Grandma never came.

Now that they're gone, I wish I could say "thank you" and "I love you" just one more time. I wish I could be good to them like they were to me and give back just a little bit of the love and joy they gave to me. I wish I could be with them, if only for a moment.

I thank God for my grandparents. What a great blessing their love and caring were for me!

I pray that my friend Leigh and others like her may also grow to love and appreciate their grandparents and that I may be a witness to that love.

Prayer: Dear Lord, thank You for the gift of grandparents—for their wisdom, their understanding, and their love. Amen.

L. G.

43

Hugs and Kisses

1 Peter 5:14

I like hugging. I feel warm and secure when I give a friend a hug of love and friendship. Hugs are ways of sharing joys and sorrows, laughter and tears. But not everybody likes hugging.

Josey was a new friend of mine whom I met at college. When it was time to say good-bye for the Christmas holidays, I hugged all my close friends. But when Josey saw me coming, she said, "If you hug me, I'll never speak to you again." Needless to say, I didn't give her a hug—although I wanted to.

About a year later, Josey and I talked about why I liked hugging and she didn't. She said that she hadn't grown up with hugs. She and her parents expressed their love for each other in other ways.

I told her why I felt that hugging is such a blessing from God. For me, a hug silently but effectively says what's in my heart. It reinforces words like "I'm sorry," "I forgive you," and "I love you." It's also an expression of joy, love, and excitement. But I told Josey, it's also something not to be forced on other people.

Last Christmas God gave me a really wonderful gift. I hugged my friend Josey . . . and she hugged me back!

Prayer: Dear Lord, give me tolerance so that I can understand and accept the different ways that people express themselves. Forgive me when I insist that my way is the only right way. And Lord, thanks for hugs. Amen.

L. G.

You Are So Good! Matt. 5:14–16

To Jessie and Eric, my dear grandchildren,

The other day I went to visit my old friend Emma. The visit was the same as any other. We talked about our children, showed each other pictures, and complained a little about getting old.

She showed me a newspaper article about a gang of young boys who beat up and robbed an old woman. "The world is going to pot," she said. "Kids are no good and getting worse all the time."

When I said that not all young people were like that, she just snorted.

Going home on the bus later that afternoon I thought about what she had said. Then I thought about you two and smiled.

This note is to say thank you—for raking the leaves, mowing the lawn, shoveling the snow, and, most of all, for taking the time to have hot chocolate and talk to a sometimes-lonely old lady.

When we talk I see your faith in your Savior and your love for Him and for me. Maybe if Emma knew some young people like you, she'd think differently about the world too.

Love,
Grandma Ruth

Prayer: Lord, make me the kind of friend who uses the opportunities You have given me to love the people around me. Amen.

L. G.

My Party . . . and No One Came

Is. 43:1, 5a.

"Life is the pits . . . war, famine, zits, and me! I must be as bad as a nuclear bomb. Put me in a room and watch it clear out. And I wear deodorant!"

"Uh, why is it that you feel this way?"

"I gave a party last Friday. Really great music and food—and my parents even promised to make themselves scarce."

"What went wrong?"

"Well, I'm not quite sure. I planned everything, invited everybody, but . . . . "

"But what?"

"But nobody came."

"Nobody?"

"Nobody! We're talkin' empty room."

"Why?"

"I don't know. Maybe everybody hates me. I'm a nobody, a zero, a loser. If you hang around me, you might become one too."

"You know, not everybody hates you. God for one. He says, 'I have summoned you by name; you are Mine.' And He says, 'Do not be afraid, for I am with you.' You know, God was at your party."

"I never thought of that. I guess He was."

Prayer: Dear Lord, at the moments in life when I am feeling like a nobody in a crowd of somebodies, help me to remember that Your love makes me precious in Your eyes, for Jesus' sake. Amen.

L. G.

New Life

Dear God,

I am feeling really confused today. I feel elated, angry, and unsure all at the same time. You know how it started, Lord. Seven months ago my mom found out she was pregnant. I was happy at first, but then I began to have second thoughts. I'd been the only child for 16 years. Would the baby rob me of my parents' love?

Well, today was the day. Sarah was born. Deep down inside I love her, and I'm really happy. But at the same time I feel cheated. Sarah's so cute, and everyone ohs and ahs over her. I feel forgotten and rejected. I guess I'm a little jealous. I don't want to feel this way—I really like little Sarah, and my head says Mom and Dad still love me.

Thank You, Lord, for being available and for paying attention to me, even when I'm not the center of everyone's attention. I feel comforted knowing that You are never too busy to deal with my questions and confusions. I know that You love me and will never let me down.

You know, I think I'm beginning to feel better already, Lord. I want to thank You for the gift of baby Sarah and the gift of new life that You gave to my family. Help me to love her and to do my part to teach her about Your love which is everlasting. Thanks for listening. Amen.

B. J. P.

Cadillac or Rusted Old V.W.?

1 Peter 2:9–10

Attention Lord:

Can You help me? I don't know what's going on with my friends lately. They've been trying to convince me to do things that I know are wrong: getting drunk, lying, swearing—you name it!

Most of the time I try to do what I know is right and stay out of trouble. When I use your strength to overcome these temptations I feel like a Cadillac—shiny clean, and meeting the quality control standards of my Maker. When they do things that are obviously wrong some of my friends seem more like rusted old V.W.'s. And sometimes I'm one, too.

Just last week my friend asked me to go with her to an all night drinking party. When I said my parents wouldn't like it she told me to lie, to tell them I was spending the night at her house. I knew it was wrong to go, but I was tempted, Lord. I didn't want her to think I was a coward, and I figured she would laugh at me if I told her that I didn't want to because I was a Christian.

You tell me in Your Word, "You are a chosen people, a royal priesthood." When I'm feeling down—like a rusted old V.W.— these words of Yours remind me that in Your eyes and through Your forgiveness, Lord, we are all Cadillacs.

Next time I feel like a rusted old V.W., or I'm tempted to act like one, help me to remember the cost of my being a Cadillac: the death and resurrection of Your son Jesus Christ. Thanks for listening, Lord. Amen.

B. J. P.

Decisions! Decisions! Prov. 3:5–6

Decisions! Decisions! Some big. Some small. Some vital. Some unimportant.

How many decisions do you make each day? And do you ever think about the decisions you make? Like, what time should you get up? Or, should you run or go swimming today?

Many daily decisions require little effort. But what about the bigger decisions? Some are really hard to face. "Do I get a job or go out for sports?" "Which college or career do I choose?" These decisions are frustrating and confusing. Sometimes they seem to take forever. Sometimes I feel like tossing up my hands and quitting.

When I face a decision, whether it's big or small, I try to remember that God is with me every step of the way and He will direct the steps I take. He has also given me special people— my parents, pastor, friends—and they can help me as I make my decisions. In any decision I make, I'm not alone. What a relief!

Prayer: Holy Lord, I have so many decisions to make. Help me to decide wisely as You walk beside me each step of the way. In Jesus' name. Amen.

B. J. P.

Away from Home

1 John 1:7

"Next!" called the woman at the desk. This was Julie's first day at college. She had already waited in five terribly long registration lines. As she waited she wondered if being away from home was always going to be as miserable as this.

"Hi, my name is Kim."

"Hi, I'm Julie."

"So, how do you like college so far?"

"Well, I'm not sure. The registration lines have been pretty dull, and I haven't really met anyone."

"Is this your first year here?"

"Sure is; how about you?"

"No," said Kim, "I was here last year. Hey, I can show you around a little later if you like. And if you want to we can have dinner together. And if you're interested you can come to church with me Sunday."

When Julie sat down alone that night she thought about the wonderful new Christian friend whom God had given her. She realized that, even though she was away from her home, family, and friends, God was always there. In fact, He was the best friend of all.

Maybe being away from home wasn't going to be so bad after all.

Prayer: Heavenly Father, thank You for always being with me, even when everything familiar seems far away. Amen.

B. J. P.

Moving Away   Luke 2:48–52

Before we were born, umbilical cords connected us to our mothers. The time came when we grew too big to live inside the womb. Our mothers endured a great amount of pain during the separation stage, but they also experienced a great amount of joy.

Teens are no longer infants, but we are still trying to break invisible umbilical cords, working toward the time when we will be independent adults—and treated as such by our parents.

As we progress through this separation stage, conflicts arise. We may feel that we are grown up enough to make our own decisions, but our parents seem to insist on treating us like small children. We believe that we're responsible young adults and deserve freedom, but our parents only seem to increase their restrictions.

The conflicts are probably inevitable, but with God's help and the fruits of the Holy Spirit we can ease the tensions between our parents and ourselves. Instead of fighting, we can choose to follow them and be obedient to them while we continue to mature physically and mentally.

Prayer: Dear Jesus, I ask for the fruits of Your Spirit—love, patience, and self-control—to help me honor and respect my parents until this separation stage is completed. Amen.

K. K.

When Things Go Wrong

Ps. 34:17–19

I stomped to my bedroom without looking back, slammed the door, and dove onto my bed. This had been the worst week of my life.

Julie and I broke up. John wouldn't speak to me because of that fight in the locker room. I failed the chemistry test, and, when I got home and told my mom, she grounded me for a week.

"God," I prayed, "why can't I do anything right? Why is my life so terrible? What am I doing wrong? Why do all of these bad things happen to me?"

Through tear-filled eyes, I caught a glimpse of a poster on my wall. "He is always with you," it said.

"At least there's one thing that won't go wrong," I thought more in self-pity than in faith.

But His Word is truth. God always loves me. No matter what happens, He's always there for me. I know that. Jesus loved me so much that He died for me. And He promises me that He will help me—through the bad times as well as the good. He is, after all, God.

Prayer: Dear God, Help me trust in Your promise that You are always with me. Strengthen my faith to believe that You will carry me through. Amen.

K. K.

What's God Have Against Me?

Matt. 6:25—34

I opened the locker room door and bounded down to the coach's office. Anticipation filled my eyes as I searched the line-up card for my name.

"Wait a second," I thought. " This has to be a mistake. Tom shouldn't start instead of me. I've worked a lot harder than he has. I live a Christian life, while he's out drinking and swearing. *My* name should be on that card. What's God have against me?"

It took a while, but finally I remembered the Christmas morning when I was six. I had wanted a toy train so badly that I cried for half an hour when I didn't get it. I thought I had done something to make God mad. I thought He really hated me. When my mom saw how upset I was, she told me that God held nothing against me; He only wanted the best for me. She reminded me that the birds of the air don't sow or reap, but God still provides for them. She told me that the lilies of the field didn't labor or spin, but God still clothes them. Then she said, "If God does all that for them, won't He give you everything you'll ever really need?"

That's a hard lesson when I hurt, but I know it's true. God doesn't hold anything against me; He loves me. When I don't get what I want, I have to remember God's wisdom: He will give me what's best for me. After all, He gave up His Son for me.

Prayer: Dear God, when I don't get what I want, help me remember that You love me and will generously provide what's best for me. Amen.

K. K.

Getting Old   Phil. 1:6

An elderly, white-haired woman shuffled up to the ice-cream stand. "How much for a medium vanilla cone?" she whispered.

"A dollar-twenty-five," I replied from behind the counter.

"What?" She asked, moving a hand to her ear.

"One dollar and a quarter," I practically shouted.

"Here's the exact change," she mumbled, handing me a dollar bill and a nickel with shaking hands.

"That's a nickel, ma'am, not a quarter," I said loudly.

"Are you sure, young man?"

"Positive."

"Let me look," she stammered. Taking the coin, she turned it over and over, close to her face. "I guess you're right," she said reaching into her purse to find a quarter for me.

Later that day as my mind wandered back to that decrepit woman, I focused on my own old age. I believe that God has a purpose for my life. I can imagine the near future and see myself glorifying the Lord with my work. But what about when I'm old? How will I be able to glorify God if I can't tell the difference between a nickel and a quarter? The prospect frightens me.

Prayer: Dear Jesus, give me the faith to believe that You have a purpose for me throughout *all* my life. Let me trust that You will continue the good work You started in me. Amen.

K. K.

Desert? I Thought You Said Dessert!

2 Cor. 12:10

Family vacations. Times for kids and parents to escape from the problems of life at home, right? Well, not necessarily. Family trips can become humorously plagued with problems.

A couple of years ago, my family took a trip that had more than its fair share of comical errors. Just a week before the well-planned drive to California, things began to fall apart. Our comfortable, one-year-old van sputtered to a stop on a highway ramp. Although mechanics promised the vehicle could be fixed in time for our vacation, complications came up, and we were forced to buy a new van just 12 hours before departure.

Car troubles fixed, and packing processes complete, we left North Carolina with optimism. Our first stop was St. Louis. My father, a pastor, was to preach a special Father's Day sermon at my grandparents' church. However, Grandpa was in the hospital with pneumonia and didn't get to hear the special sermon.

I could go on with details about food poisoning, rain storms, rustic cabins, and stolen car keys. But that's not my point. Even in the disappointments, there were good times, fond memories, and celebrations.

Life often feels like a desert, filled with problems too hot to be solved. But God reminds us that He puts sweet things into life as well. Even when life seems extremely bad, we can always find God's desserts scattered around in the midst of our deserts.

Prayer: Dear Lord, thank You for the special things in my life. Help me to see beyond the desert of life and on to the oasis of Your love. Amen.

C. R.

Remembering Water   Rom. 6:3–4

I remember with great clarity the crisp October day that my family hiked the Blue Ridge Mountains. We bundled up in warm sweaters and jackets to keep out the chill.

After walking for nearly an hour through silent woods, we found a cascading stream that crossed the trail. Attempting to reach the other side, I dropped my left foot into the middle of the cold, swiftly flowing stream. Unfortunately, my old sneakers didn't hold on the slick rocks, and I fell into the icy water.

No roller coaster ride anywhere compares to the splashing slalom that followed. Panicking, I grabbed at the rocks to my left and right, but couldn't find a thing to hold on to. My slide down the stream finally ended in a small pool between two large rocks. Soaking wet and feeling a little humbled, I climbed out of the freezing water amid rounds of applause from my parents and brother.

Life is much the same way. All people fall short of God's glory because the stream of sin knocks us off balance and continues to pull us away from Him. We slip and slide, unable to grab hold ourselves, unable to keep from sinning. But God is ready to catch us. God cleanses us from all the sin which draws us away from Him, and He makes us His precious children in the special water of our baptism.

Prayer: Dear Lord, always be there to catch me when I fall. Amen.

C. R.

Detours

Prov. 15:33

The piano bench squeaked as I drew it in toward my knees and sat down. My heart pounded. I realized that my first music competition was now a reality.

My fingers touched the keys, and the Mozart sonata flowed freely from my memory. Finishing the complicated succession of trills and scales, I ended with one triumphant chord. Walking back to my comforting seat in the audience, I smiled contentedly and reassured myself that no one— not even Mozart—deserved first place as much as I did.

As an independent person, I left humility behind. I felt I had everything under control. I had given the performance of a lifetime, and it must be rewarded with first prize.

My pride became my folly. My faith got detoured. I didn't even receive an honorable mention. My pride made me lose sight of reality.

As I look back on my performance, I know I used my musical skills to the level of my ability as God had blessed my studies. *That* was reason to celebrate. There's no better reward then to know God has helped me do my best—even if that's not award-winning.

Prayer: Dear Lord, pride can become a detour and obstacle as I live each day. I pray, Lord, that You would grant me wisdom to follow Your lead and to use the gifts You have given me— not that I be honored, but that You be glorified. Amen.

C. R.

Nicknames

Prov. 22:1

Blubber, String Bean, Turkey, Whale—
Nicknames we've all heard before.
Chubby, Stubby, Bones, and Nerd—
Just to add a couple more.
At school, at home, and work as well,
People use some awful names.
Little do they understand
How they hurt with nickname games.
Understanding hurt and pain,
God knows how it feels, you see.
For some awful names were called
When He died on Calvary.
God has given you a name,
One which stands above the rest.
You are called *a chosen child,*
Named in love and richly blessed.
When in heaven you arrive
And are seated with the Son,
No more nicknames will be called,
For you are God's own special one.

Prayer: Dear Lord, help me to live in Your light with the knowledge that You love me. Amen.

C. R.

Memo

A grandma is special whether she enjoys rocking chairs or plays tennis. She tells you how special you are too, what great things you can accomplish, and raves at all your efforts no matter how feeble.

Growing old is growing in wisdom, and a grandma can be surprisingly understanding. She knows what the latest fashion is and why you either want to build muscles or be thin and cur-vaceous. She remembers your special days even if you forget hers. Tell her about your grades, and she'll recall how your dad or mom did in high school. She listens carefully to all you say when you're in the pits and pouring out your heart.

Then there's Grandma's faith. Lois, believing in the power of our Lord, passed her faith on to her daughter Eunice and, through her, her grandson Timothy. So it can be for you too.

Treasure your grandma. She is a gift from God who will love you regardless of your funny hair-do's, your picky appetites, your mood swings, your opinionated moments, your ego trips.

Prayer: "My son [daughter], do not forget my teaching, but keep my commands in your heart. . . . Trust in the Lord with all your heart and lean not on your own understanding" (Prov. 3:1, 5). Amen.

B. W. D.

Sisters

Luke 10:38-39

"Hey, Mother, she's making me late again!" She must be the slowest person on earth; school only starts the same time each day.

"We can't go to the movies," I say. "It was your turn to clean our room, but you didn't do it." Her fault again.

"Mother, she wore my new scarf, and I bought it especially for the football game." She louses up everything!

One of these days, as soon as I'm grown-up, I'll disown her.

* * * * *

That was a long time ago, and I know now why God made sisters. They can be your best friends. They love you when you're super and when you're not so super. They hug you and go on for hours about little things, like the simple birthday card you bought. And when you're the oldest, like I am, they'll even listen to your advice, prize it like the Hope Diamond, and even pass it on to others. (This, of course, helps older sisters keep walking the straight and narrow.)

Before, during, and after I decided I did or did not need something, God saw my needs—and one was a sister. Everyday I thank God for the great gift she is to me.

Prayer: Father, thank You so much for all the trivia it takes for us to appreciate the best in those we call "a pain." As Jesus cares for us as brothers and sisters, may we do likewise for our earthly sisters and brothers. Amen.

B. W. D.

Nine and Countin'

Nine months ago I was having fun.
All that's ended, and Bud's on the run.
Mom and Dad said it would be this way;
No dates, no parties, no friends come to stay.
No allowance, it now buys formula instead.
Crying, diapers, screaming, bottles, barfing, laundry—
Exhausted, I go to bed.
Hey, World, life was never supposed to be like this.
You've turned the tables. Life's a mess.
You promised the pill, abortion, safe sex;
You failed me. Something didn't work;
You X'd out all the pleasures.
You did a "no stop, no return."
I turned a deaf ear to everyone.
Like Adam and Eve I've taken the fall.
My inner being screams,
"Somebody help! Let me out of here!"
No one answers; no one cares.
I sit in silence and in fear.
Nearby my Bible sits, unused and new,
In deep despair I pick it up for some resolving clue.

And there I read: "Let us then approach the throne of grace with confidence, so that we may receive mercy and find grace to help us in our time of need" (Heb. 4:16). Amen.

B. W. D.

God's Hall of Fame Ps. 41:3

Grace was ill long before any of us knew. And when we did find out, everything she probably feared happened. We cried and she said, "Don't." We moped and she said, "Cheer up; we'll make the best of what our Lord has given us."

Had God given us something we couldn't see? What we were seeing certainly was not a gift we could easily appreciate: our loving, active, involved friend was being consumed by the destructive parasite, cancer. Yet, Grace became our tower of strength, giving us her very best every day.

Music had been her lifelong love. There had been plays to direct, dramas to cast, recitals to prepare. This was the 33d anniversary of one of her choral groups.

Grace set about writing letters to invite friends to the coming event. She and a caterer prepared a menu. Programs were printed, music was selected, and rehearsals began.

Her suffering was consuming us, but she affirmed, "God is my comfort; He's been my physician when I thought the pain would be unbearable."

Grace spent a week in the hospital, then asked the doctor's permission to return home to complete the necessary preparations for the program, two weeks away. Greeting visitors from her bed, her strength of will remained obvious.

When the final chorus was sung and the last bit of punch poured, the sandwich plate was empty—and so was Grace's bed.

Prayer: O God, whom in affliction I call my comfort, my hope, my salvation, be with me this day. Amen.

B. W. D.

Algebra—Help!

Binomials, constants, quadratic equations, irrational numbers. Familiar terms, right? Most teens have had the pleasure of experiencing the wonderful, complicated, sometimes seemingly incomprehensible world of algebra.

But I can think of something really impossible to understand: God. Do we realize that He sacrificed His only Son so we could live? And do we know why He did this? Because He loves us. Of course, we tell ourselves, we'd do the same if we were in His shoes.

Oh, sure we would! It makes a lot of sense to sacrifice the one we love the most for a world that barely notices.

But whoever said God had to make sense? We just need to be filled with His love and peace, and He sends His Holy Spirit to accomplish that in us. The Spirit helps us believe and trust, even when we cannot understand Him.

In algebra we get a good grade by mastering the subject matter. In God we get salvation for free, even if we don't comprehend the love that went into our salvation.

But it doesn't pay to get technical with God. We don't have to score good grades to please Him. He's pleased when we just accept what He's putting in our hands.

Prayer: Dear Lord, make my heart and mind receptive to Your Holy Spirit so I may grow more confident of Your love for me. In Your name. Amen.

A. B.

Are You a Problem?   1 Peter 5:8

In a recent interview, the Devil shared a few thoughts on the matter of young people. He explained that youth are easily turned into troublemakers. They are unsure about faith and God. This makes them easy targets for temptation. Once they commit a sin, it's easy to make them feel guilty and depressed.

"Isn't it great?" (At least that's what the Devil said.) "Another great tactic to lead young ones into sin," he continued, "is to make them feel worthless. It's just a little game I play. The various reactions I get from teens is quite entertaining."

But God also has a few thoughts on the subject. He encourages, "Don't let anyone look down on you because you are young, but set an example for the believers in speech, in life, in love, in faith and in purity" (1 Tim. 4:12). God also reassures, "We are his people, the sheep of his pasture" (Ps. 100:3). Even when we mess up, God loves us and renews us. "Even youths grow tired and weary, and young men stumble and fall; but those who hope in the Lord will renew their strength. They will soar on wings like eagles; they will run and not grow weary, they will walk and not be faint" (Is. 40:30–31).

Trust in God. You're not a problem to Him; you're His child.

Prayer: Dearest Jesus, sometimes I feel worthless and unlovable. I cause so many problems for everyone. Please remind me that You don't make junk, and that I'm a saved, chosen person too. Help me to work out my problems and amend my mess-ups. For Your love and forgiveness, I pray. Amen.

A. B.

PIG-OUT! Prov. 23:19–25

PIZZA, COOKIES 'N' CREAM, BANANA SPLITS, CORN CHIPS, SODA, MALTS.

Have you ever felt the urge to open your mouth wide and scoop every edible thing into it in one big munch? God provides delightful delicacies for us to eat, so why not eat all of them at once? Right?

Wrong! Common sense tells us this is bad for health reasons. Our bodies simply can't burn that many calories all at once. But what do you care about health when you are in the midst of savoring those delectable concoctions?

God provides us with reasons for not binging or purging. He says we were created in His likeness and are now His spiritually, mentally, and physically. He expects us to keep our bodies, His temples, neat and in good working order. He also expects us not to abuse the abundance of food He blesses us with. As we are good stewards of our bodies—healthy, strong, and able—so they will serve us well.

The Bible says God bought us, our bodies and souls, at a very dear price: His holy, precious Son. When you read the words, "Honor God with your body," think of them as loving advice from God, your concerned Friend.

Prayer: Thanks God, for gifts of food You provide for me. Please strengthen my self-control so I will not abuse these gifts. In Your name I pray. Amen.

A. B.

The All Night Horror Show

Rom. 6:23

You're alone. Completely alone. Except for that laugh.

A hideous screeching laugh. Surrounding you. Engulfing you. Then comes the fire. In front of you. Behind you. Below you. There's no escape. Stop the laugh, but it has no source. Quench the fire, but you have no water. Give up, but there's no surrender. You have nothing going for you.

But you're *not* alone. Now you're comforted, and the comfort is love. The source is God who was standing by you through it all. As quickly as waking from a nightmare the horror stops, and the reality of His strong love is hugging you close.

Everyone has those horrid nights, sweaty and chilling at the same time. They make the movies seem like kindergarten stuff and the videos like child's play. For this is your own personal horror show, and you feel godforsaken.

But you're not. Not since that real nightmare on the Friday called Good when Jesus screamed out, "My God, my God, why have you forsaken me?" Because He was forsaken, we never will be.

Prayer: Dear Jesus, Your love for me guarantees: Heaven's open; hell's shut. Open my eyes so I can see through the Devil's nightmares to focus on Your open-armed invitation to love and life eternal. I praise You for opening heaven wide by Your death and resurrection. You live, and now so do I. Thanks be to God! Amen.

A. B.

Do We Really Want to Be Modern People? 1 Cor. 6:9–11

Julie walked into Kim's party hoping to have a good time with her friends. Music was blaring as she looked around. Beer cans were everywhere. There was a full bar. Powders, pills, bags of grass, and cigarette papers littered the coffee table.

Julie wandered down the hall to put her purse in Kim's room. She slowly opened the door and saw Kim and Tom lying on the bed. She closed the door, walked out, and left the party.

Sex and drugs just weren't for Julie. Why should they be? She is a Christian, and she wants to do what pleases the Lord. God says, "Do you not know that the wicked will not inherit the kingdom of God?" That Bible passage also tells us that sex for the fun of it and getting drunk or high are plain wrong.

Our modern society certainly tests what we believe as God's people, but we don't have to go along. God gives us a way out through His Son, Jesus Christ. He forgives what we have done and gives us strength to resist evil in the future. He offers a new way of living and of having fun. Let's not change His ways to suit the world. Let's call on His name, and His power, to change our world to please Him!

Prayer: Dear Father, so often it's easier to give in, to be like the world. Help me to be more like You, to live in Your love, and to enjoy friends and fun that please You. Amen.

C. J.

Temples Are Sacred   1 Cor. 3:16–17

My friend Kelli and I were at the amusement park, walking along, talking, trying to decide what ride to go on, when two guys approached us. They asked us if we'd like to go on the Ferris wheel with them. They seemed nice enough, so we agreed. One of the guys asked Kelli if she partied. Kelli said, "Sure!"

I never knew Kelli partied. She was always the Christian friend I counted on. We went to church together. Kelli, a party-hearty?

The guy sitting near Kelli pulled out a cigarette, lit it, took a puff, and offered it to Kelli. As she took it, I leaned closer. Funny looking cigarette—with twisted ends. Funny smell too. Kelli took her hit on the joint and passed it on to the other guy. She knew better than to pass it to me.

I never thought one of my close Christian friends would do drugs. She knew how I felt. Our bodies are God's temples. We're sacred to Him. Hurting ourselves means destroying His temples. It's not only dumb, it really hurts the Lord.

God hates the destruction of what He has made, but He offers, by His grace, restoration. We can be rebuilt through the death and resurrection of Jesus Christ. God's ready to forgive, to make us His sacred dwelling places again.

Prayer: Heavenly Father, help me to think as much of myself as You do. You made me, then remade me in Jesus Christ. I am Your temple. Live in me that I may always live in You. Amen.

C. J.

Scars Removed

My dear friend,

I need to share with you the new direction my life has taken.

Remember how I was down all the time before? I never told you, but my father's an alcoholic. I felt ashamed about it—like it was my fault. I felt afraid and alone, especially at home. The night Dad smashed the television I knew I was losing it.

The next day at school a girl came up to me. She told me she knew how I felt and that God didn't want me to feel that way.

I knew about God's love and all that, and even prayed a little. It never seemed to help. But now I think He answered my prayers through her. She told me about God's love again and prayed with me—only this time it felt real. She shared a Bible passage to help me: "Hope does not disappoint us" (Rom. 5:5). That verse hit home. I took the Bible she offered me and went home that day feeling different.

For the first time in a long time I had joy and hope inside me. It was as if a door had been unlocked and the love of God came pouring in.

When Dad came home drunk again, I no longer felt alone. God was with me. He helped me forgive Dad, just as He had forgiven me.

I love my dad, but now I'm not ashamed. Now I hope he can know the joy God has brought me. I hope you can feel it too. You don't need a problem like mine before you come to Him. God just wants to be your friend—always. So do I.

C. J.

Go!

Jesus says to His Church, "Go and make disciples of all nations" (Matt. 28:19). Great! How can we do that? Trained pastors, teachers, and other missionaries go abroad with their families each year to teach people in foreign countries that Jesus died and rose again for each of us.

That's great for people who can spend years learning a foreign language and living in another country. But what about me, a teenager, here in the United States? How can I "go"?

Jesus said something else very important. He told His disciples in Acts 1 to be His witnesses in Jerusalem, Judea, Samaria, and to the ends of the earth. But He mentioned Jerusalem first. That was the disciples' hometown. Get the picture? *We can start to go by staying put.*

Witnessing for Jesus doesn't just happen in mud huts and jungles somewhere across an ocean. It happens wherever we are. He opens the doors for us to go. We go by our words and our actions and our service to others. And He goes with us, always. Each command of our Lord also brings with it a promise of His forgiveness, strength, and love. That gives us the go-power to live and witness for Him.

So—let's go!

Prayer: Jesus, give me the courage to speak Your name and tell Your story. Keep my eyes and ears open for opportunities to go for You. Thanks for all Your love for me! Amen.

C. J.

Sherry Smiled
1 Cor. 10:17

Sherry didn't smile often. She had been abused by her dad, so she had lived with an aunt for three years. Then her best friend Kim was killed in a car accident. Sherry didn't have much to smile about.

Then God touched her life. After Kim died, Sherry had prayed for a new friend. God didn't give her just one friend however; He gave her three friends. She met them at church camp, and they grew together like sisters. But her new friends lived far away. So Sherry smiled a little more, but not much. She prayed to be with her new friends more often, trusting God's power to make it happen.

One day while studying about Holy Communion for confirmation class, she realized something fantastic: every time she and her friends took communion, even in their different churches, it would be as if they were kneeling at the same altar. Christ Himself joined them as "one body" by their faith in His promises of forgiveness and hope. She couldn't wait to be confirmed.

That's when Sherry smiled. God had brought her through the pain and blessed her with a very special link to her new friends through the gift of His Son and His Supper.

Prayer: Lord, help me treasure Your Supper. Remind me of Your forgiving power and the joy of being one in You. Amen.

R. L.

Transformers
Rom. 12:1–2

A recent headline in a cheap tabloid read, "Woman Turns Into Cat After Eating Cat Food For Twenty Years." According to the old saying "you are what you eat," but that story is hard to swallow!

Still whatever we take into ourselves will have some effect on us—whether we eat it, breathe it, or touch it. Smoking can destroy our lungs. Drugs and alcohol damage brain cells. Even suntanning can cause skin cancer. These things are obvious. But many teens don't realize that what we watch, read, and listen to also affects us.

Choices of books, magazines, music, and television are based on what everybody else likes. But "everybody" can be wrong. Not everything out there is good. When it comes to entertainment a better gauge of good or bad might be, "Would I enjoy sharing that with God?"

There's no need to accept everything the world shoves at us. Rather, God has challenged us to avoid conformity. We are transformed from dying sinners into living members of His family. We are a part of His divine plan, blessed in love, forgiveness, and power. The Christian life is a new life of hope and blessing—the best kind of life.

Prayer: Lord, so often I fit the pattern of this sinful world. I act now and think later. I wrongly assume I can stand up to the bad things and won't be affected. Help me to desire what You want and to make choices that please You, for Your love's sake. Amen.

R. L.

.The Big Bang Theory

1 Thess. 4:16–18

"Hey, Johnny, speak to me! Tell me again how you think a total nuclear war can be won. There won't be anything left!"

"Stay cool, Steve. I'm just repeating what Mike said. He's the expert."

"Let's have a word with Einstein then," Steve exclaimed.

They found Mike coming out of the chapel, starting toward the cafeteria. Steve and Johnny laid out their dispute for him.

"Well, you see," Mike replied, "if the world does end with a big bang, it will be the greatest victory for the Lord. I call it my Big Bang Theory."

"Doesn't that theory explain how the world began?" asked Steve.

"Not in my book," Mike countered. "Anyway, there's more to my theory. It seems to me that God won't let men take away what He made. I believe He'll bring about the end of the world in some other way—His way.

"Whether this planet blows up or becomes a poisoned wasteland or runs out of food, the result will be the same for believers. All who trust in Jesus Christ will live with Him forever.

"In the meantime, how about some breakfast?"

Prayer: Lord, give me the confidence to know that how I think the world might end isn't nearly as important as how I trust in You right now. Forgive my needless worry, and give me courage to witness to Your everlasting truth. Amen.

R. L.

Reunions

"I'm hoping this year you'll be more friendly to your cousins," Tim's mom said from the front seat of the car. "Every year you're more withdrawn at these reunions. Why don't you make an effort to enjoy your family?"

Tim didn't answer. He just watched the pine trees chase each other past the car window. He missed his girlfriend. He missed his stereo. He was missing the trip to the lake with the guys. He was trapped, and he had decided to be miserable.

For a teen with his own interests, family reunions can be a real bummer.

Perhaps it's not till we're older that we can really appreciate what a reunion is all about. The family can give us a sense of where we come from, what our ancestry is, what our heritage is. It sounds pretty dusty, but it doesn't have to be.

God put people in families. He gave family members to each other to love, cherish, and nurture, but also to celebrate, play, and pray with. Families are gifts from God—maybe not always easily appreciated, but as Jacob said to Esau, "They are the [family] God has graciously given your servant."

Prayer: Lord, when I think only of what is important to me, I cheat myself of many of Your blessings. Thank You for families and for reunions with those You have given to me. Amen.

R. L.

Smiles

> If you're happy and you know it,
> Then your face will surely show it.
> If you're happy and you know it,
> Shout amen. Amen!

Does your face give any indication of what you believe? A smile expresses outwardly what is on the inside.

I find that a smile excellently expresses the joy of God's unending love and forgiveness. And why not smile? If you had been the only person in the world who had sinned, Jesus would have come and died for you alone.

I didn't realize the impact a smile can have on others until I spent several days with a group of Christian people I had never met before. Anyone could tell a great deal about us by looking at our faces. We shared a lot of special times and became close friends within a few days.

One newfound friend made a lasting impression by something she said. She told me that my smile would get me through many of the hard times of my life.

Well, she proved right quicker than she could have thought. Even though I was sad as I got on the plane to come home from the gathering, I could smile with a deep joy.

Prayer: Father, there will be days on which it seems impossible to smile. Help me not to make excuses, but remind me of the real reason to smile: Christ, my risen Lord. Amen.

C. W.

From the Ground Up   Matt. 7:24–27

"And the house and the sand went smash!" says a song about two men. A wise man built his house on a rock and a foolish man built on the sand. After a storm the house on the rock was still standing, but the house on the sand had been washed away. A later verse of that song talks about building life on Jesus Christ.

Obviously, a good house must be firmly anchored to solid ground. And just as obviously, a custom job takes time to complete.

These principles also apply to people. A person whose foundation is Jesus Christ will successfully endure life's storms. In addition, God has His own construction schedule and individual blueprints for each person.

Prayer: Father, help me to be patient, realizing that Your work as the Master Carpenter is an ongoing project in me. My heart always needs to be repaired. Some days it's shattered like a pane of window glass. Sometimes it's like a locked door, keeping my mind from accepting others' ideas. At other times, the shutters of my heart are closed, preventing the light of Your love from touching a friend's need. Help me to be patient with myself and with other people, realizing we are all under construction. In the name of Jesus, who died on a great piece of wood. Amen.

C. W.

Contentjealousyment

Heb. 13:5

Why does everyone else get what I want? The clothes, the car, the job, the friends, the grades, the lead part, the solo. They win and I lose. Are they any better, smarter, more talented, or more deserving than I am? It sure seems that way.

I don't know what it is, God, but I'm ready to give up and quit. Isn't it my turn to be number one? I hope being jealous is just part of growing up; but whether or not, I'm jealous now. I know it's wrong—maybe that's why I'm talking to You about it.

I know I have talents. I try to get involved in things so that I can use my abilities. Sure, I like the credit, but that isn't the only reason. You have told me to use my talents, not hide them. But then someone else gets the part, makes the team, or is selected for choir, band, or class office. And I get nothing.

That's why I'm jealous. I don't even get to use my talents when I try. It just isn't fair that someone else is always the winner.

I can't lie to You, God. It's mostly my pride, Lord. Take away the bitter hurt and jealousy inside me so that I can sincerely congratulate others.

Prayer: God, grant me the patience to keep looking for the special part You have created just for me. And in the meantime, help with my jealousy. Help me to learn to be more content with who I am and with what You have given me. In the name of Jesus, who made each and every one of us winners in Your sight. Amen.

C. W.

The Rat Race of Life   Heb. 12:1

Would you run a 100-meter race wearing 10-pound ankle weights? Of course not.

In the marathon of life many people do strap on weights— guilt, grudges, and sorrow. I realize that I can't run successfully in my race while I'm carrying my sins, but it's hard to shed them once they're on.

A special friend pointed out to me that Christ was strong enough to bear the all world's sins on the cross. So He can help me to become free of hindrances in my life.

"Spiritually I am not a super athlete. How can I run this race?"

"This race is different; to win, you only have to finish."

"But what if I fall down and can't finish the race?"

"Remember that Jesus is by your side to help you each and every step of the way. Let him help carry your burdens."

"Is it too late to enter this race?"

"No, you're running by just being alive."

"I don't understand everything about this race called life, but I'm beginning to see that God cares about me and will help me with my running. That's enough for now."

Prayer: Father, help me cast aside life's burdens as I run in Your race. Guide me around obstacles which are too high to hurdle. In all things lead me toward Your prize of heaven. In the name of Your Son, Jesus Christ, who died and rose again. Amen.

C. W.

Inside, Outside

With my first step into the new school I could feel the strange students' stares bore into me. I could imagine what they were saying.

"Who's she?"

"Where did she come from?"

"Is that the new girl? She's kind of ugly."

"What kind of clothes are those? She's got no sense of style."

I could see them pointing at and stereotyping me.

"She looks like a wimp!"

"She seems to be a straight-A student."

Inwardly I cringed at all these conclusions being drawn about me. They didn't know what kind of person I was inside. They had no right to do this to me! But outwardly I held my head high and kept smiling.

I always knew this would happen to me sooner or later—because I have done it to others. At times I've looked at a new face and thought, "What a snob," without first getting to know the person. After all these years of passing judgment, I now understand what those other people went through.

Prayer: Dear Lord, ever patient, ever loving, I finally understand. Please forgive me for judging others. You don't care what we look like. You judge us by what's inside our hearts. Thank You for being so kind; help me learn to be the same. In Jesus' name. Amen.

J. H.

A Jubilant Song   Eph. 5:19–20

My town's annual Spring Concert is an important event for my church choir. All the church choirs in our town gather to praise the Lord in song and celebrate the life He has given us.

We spend months preparing for the concert, going over the music until we know it perfectly. We learn how the director wants us to sing, what emotion each song is to convey.

By concert day we only have to set up risers at the high school and run through a last minute rehearsal. Finally everything is ready for that night. It's hard work, but it's worth the effort. It's our way of thanking God for life.

Of the many ways of praising God, music has to be the most joyful. I love its way of showing Him how much I care by sharing His love with others. Through music I can spread God's Word by joyfully using the talent He has given me. And, for me, music is a way to say, "Lord, I'm glad You're here."

One neat part about music is that even if you're not in a choir or very talented, you still can sing praises to God with all your heart.

Prayer: Dear Lord, You give us everything we need. We thank You especially for the gift of jubilant song with which to praise You. Help us to use all of our abilities to glorify Your name. Teach us to show the joy Your love brings to us. In Jesus' name. Amen.

J. H.

I've Got to Be Me   1 Cor. 12:4

Mike could feel all eyes on him as he walked off the court. He painfully recalled the last seconds of the game: A kid had run up to him, grabbed the ball away, and made the winning basket.

Mike smacked his forehead thinking, "Why was I so dumb? I froze; I just watched him take the ball away. Why did I join the basketball team in the first place? It's definitely not me. But all the other guys were joining, and I didn't want to be left out."

Dejected, Mike walked into the music room and sat down at the piano. He took out the song he was composing and proceeded to lose himself in a world of music.

Later he laughed, "If only the guys could see me now." Trying to cheer himself up he thought, "I'm no basketball star— but God loves me anyway. So why does it matter? Well, I'll just have to show them at tomorrow's concert where my talent really lies. If they're my true friends, they'll stand by me."

The next night Mike could see his friends' bemused expressions as he got up on stage and announced, "I'm going to play a song I composed." He turned to the piano and his fingers flew over the keys. When he finished, all was silent for a moment. Then there was loud applause. And Mike's friends were standing, leading the ovation!

"Lord," Mike thought, "thank You."

Prayer: Dear Lord, giver of all gifts, teach us to trust in You and be ourselves. Help us to be proud of who we are as Your children. In Jesus' name. Amen.

J. H.

On Loan

How do you deal with the death of someone you love?

I grappled with that when my cousin died. I didn't know what to do or where to turn for help. I thought that Kevin went into the hospital for appendicitis. The next thing I knew, my aunt called to tell us that he had died. When an autopsy was done, we learned Kevin had had acute leukemia. He was only 15.

For a while after his death, I felt angry with God. I didn't understand why He had taken away someone we loved. But I realized that God also loved Kevin. Then I remembered what my aunt had said: "I guess God only lets us borrow them for a while."

I thought about this for a long time and realized how true it is. We all are God's children. For a time He puts us into other people's lives to help, understand, and love. But finally we go to our true home.

Not that God wanted people to die. Death is the result of sin in the world. But through the death and resurrection of His Son Jesus, God has defeated sin. He takes us home, where we all truly belong, with Him in heaven.

We on earth may mourn, balancing our hurt with remembrances of a special person. But we thank God for the home to which that person has gone.

Prayer: Dear Lord, creator of life, please help us to understand Your love and to find hope when we lose people we love. Please give us strength in our time of mourning, and joy in the promise of heaven. In Jesus' name. Amen.

J. H.

Dad Says, "Study More!"

Matt. 7:9–12

We often say one thing when we really mean something else:

Dad: "How come you got a C in English when you're capable of doing A work?"

Daughter: "That course was really tough, and the teacher gave us a lot of work."

Dad: "Well, why didn't you work harder?"

Daughter: "Why bother? C is average, and that's good enough."

Things become much clearer when we say what is in our hearts:

Dad: "I love you and want the best for you. Working for good grades now will equip you to face problems in adult life. I wish I had worked harder when I was your age."

Daughter: "Dad, I *am* trying though I probably could have done better. But I have a lot of things going on, and it's hard to balance them all."

Truth is, we both have a lot of learning to do, building mutual trust to express our real feelings about ourselves and our concerns for one another. Thank goodness our love and care for each other allows us to keep working at it.

Prayer: Dear Father, we thank You that Your perfect love and concern for us has saved us from our biggest failure: our own sin. Please help us to listen for the meaning behind our words so that we can help each other through life. In Jesus' name. Amen.

R. L.

He Speaks Through Me!

Matt. 10:19–20

I've always considered myself to be shy. It's tough enough to carry on a conversation with a stranger who asks me a question. It's really hard to begin a conversation with the purpose of explaining the hope I have through my Lord and Savior Jesus Christ.

I have my fears: I don't know what to say . . . my faith isn't strong enough . . . my tongue will get tangled . . . people will laugh at me. My fears are hard to overcome, but I do keep trying. And I do have help.

That's the marvelous thing about our loving God. You'd think it would be enough to give His only Son up to death, to suffer and die as a payment for the sins of people like me. He even raised Jesus from the dead, promising that I also will inherit eternal life because of His Son.

Yet He does even more, sending His Holy Spirit to speak through believers—even through the likes of me! The more I study His Word, the deeper my faith is grounded in understanding. All the time the Holy Spirit is at work helping me to know what to say, willing to speak through me, and calming my fears.

Oh, I'm not ready to stand on street corners and face complete strangers. But I can let the light of God's love shine in my life and let it be a conversation starter. And the right words will come.

Prayer: Holy Spirit, deepen my faith and understanding of God's love. Cause that love to shine through me and use me to tell of it. In Jesus' name. Amen.

R. L.

Government—Does It Just Happen?

Matt. 22:21

Sometimes I feel so powerless to influence what goes on around me. Government seems blind to my needs and concerns. It seems like politicians only want to look out for themselves and are insensitive to the little guy.

Then I remember Lincoln's description of our "government of the people, by the people, for the people." I am called, in fact, to participate in my government.

As a Christian I have a lot to give to Caesar. At the minimum, I can pay my taxes as Jesus said. I also can vote for leaders who pledge to make government function for the good of the people. I can write to my congressman so he is aware of the concerns of those he represents. I can apply my beliefs in seeking to encourage sensitive, responsible government for my city, state and country. I can participate in local citizen's groups or even run for office myself.

Prayer: Dear Lord, sometimes it's too easy to blame others, excusing myself as being too young, too old, too poor, too powerless to have my voice heard. Help me remember, first, that I am important to You, and that You hear my cries. Then help me to act as a Christian to serve others, even as I pay my taxes, vote, or participate in government myself. Amen.

R. L.

When Times Get Rough Prov. 17:17

When the economy falters even in a great country there are cruel realities: businesses go bankrupt, farms are repossessed, people lose jobs. The head of a household needs to provide adequate food, shelter, and clothing. But when this is not possible, feelings of failure, guilt, shame, hopelessness, and anger may easily develop.

These are times to share the burdens. These are times to call on friends—or to be friends.

Be sure of one thing: Problems are not punishment from God. He already took care of punishment when He vented His anger at our sins by allowing His own Son to be punished.

So Jesus is your first Friend. He is crying with you. He shares the hurt. He wants to carry the burden for you. Give it to Him. Trust Him to help and comfort.

Because His Holy Spirit lives in believers, they also care for you. So give your burden to a friend too. The weight of bad feelings will be lighter when you share. The outlook will be brighter when you have help to face today—and the future.

You also have the privilege of being a friend. While bad things may not be happening to you, someone else may be trying to deal with difficulties right now. Your listening ear, your concern, your willingness to help are just what someone else needs.

Prayer: Dear Jesus, our first Friend, the cares of this world weigh me down. They are so hard to carry! Take them from me and walk beside me to listen and lead as I seek my direction and find my hope in You. Amen.

R. L.

Stickman Smiles   Eph. 6:14–16

Here in New York City I've seen a lot of strange people over the years, but none as odd as a high-schooler named Stickman.

Strange as it seems, tall, slim Stickman looked as if he was made out of wood. Even though he appeared to be nothing more than a walking branch, he was really a fine, happy young man. But no one took the time to notice that except me.

As you may have guessed, being that different caused many problems for the poor guy. He was the butt of many jokes. His classmates referred to him as "bark brain" and "termite tantalizer." No one cared about what he was like inside.

Amazingly, Stickman withstood all the cruel comments and still stayed happy. It didn't seem to bother him. One day I asked why.

He told me, "My ability to remain happy and joyful in such dreary situations rests in God's love for me." Then he quoted the verses from Ephesians about using God as a shield from evil.

Stickman had great confidence in the Lord, and through the Lord he had achieved confidence in himself. "After all," Stickman said, "God loves me, and God is the best friend anyone could have."

Prayer: Lord, sometimes others treat me like Stickman. Help me understand that You have made each one of us special, and that You have given me beautiful gifts, including protection from evil. Help me learn a new respect for others and for myself. Thank You, dear Lord. Amen.

C. L.

I'm Not God

Ps. 37:23–24

Life is not easy, especially not for me. I do everything wrong. Even my name is wrong—Elvis Jones. Can you believe that? My mother named me after her favorite rock 'n' roll star.

I do everything wrong. I can even imagine coming home from school (after failing a major history test) and stepping on some lady's pet cockroach. (How many screwballs do you know that own pet cockroaches?) Well, the lady would call my parents who would immediately ground me. Then my girlfriend, a pro-cockroach activist, would dump me. Even my friends wouldn't talk to me. (They wouldn't be able to stop laughing.)

The things that *really* happen to me seem just as ridiculous. Everyone gets on my case because I sometimes do the wrong thing. Well, I am not perfect. I am not God.

Yet, with all my problems, I have found something amazing: God has chosen me to be one of His own, and I am loved. More important than all my faults, failures, and foibles is my faith in the Lord. In Him, I have a purpose: to serve and praise Him. And I'll trust Him to take care of the rest—to see a loser as a winner!

Prayer: Heavenly Father, help me realize that I am a winner through Your amazing grace and love. I thank You for this and ask Your help as I try to show others the love You have for us all. In Your Son's name. Amen.

C. L.

Come On In

Eph. 2:12–13, 19

Life in the streets is bad. Johnnie knows. He has spent most of his life trying to survive what he calls "the torture and suffering of the street" with no home, nothing to eat, and winter cold that makes you wish you could die.

Johnnie used to curse God for his life of suffering. He kept asking why God was torturing him; he didn't deserve it.

One night Johnnie stumbled into an old church. The pastor there took the time to listen to Johnnie's questions, to offer Jesus' words of care and support, and to help Johnnie find a job.

He found work in a lumber company and got off the streets. Though it doesn't pay much, Johnnie is eating regularly and has his own place now.

"God was always with me," Johnnie says. "God was just waiting for the moment when I could hear Him calling. He didn't bring about my torment; that's the way of the sinful earth. God was the One who delivered me from sin. I know that now. There was always a place for me in the house of the Lord; it just took someone to offer me an invitation."

Prayer: Dear God, thank You for the comfort and protection which You provide for me. Without You, I am at the mercy of sin and the devil. Keep me safe from harm and danger, and stay with me forever. Amen.

C. L.

There Goes My Life   2 Tim. 1:3–4

Love is a powerful emotion. When someone feels love for another, the world becomes a wonderful place. Each person gives to the other without limit or regret. Often they build their worlds around one another. Love is a mutual desire to share and to please.

But what if the person you care most about moves away? How can you be happy when the most important person in your life is gone? You can spend a lot of money on phone calls and stamps, but that's a poor substitute for being together. Visits are expensive and in some cases impossible.

Some people feel as though a piece of their body has been ripped away.

Yet, whatever the reason for the separation, both the ones moving and the ones left behind grieve and must rebuild their worlds.

That's not impossible. Jesus is there to lend a helping hand. You cannot play baseball with Him, and He may not make you feel like your loved one might have; but He does care about how you feel, and He does provide you with His continuing love. He is a friend who will never leave, a friend who is always there.

Prayer: Dearest Jesus, help me in dealing with the absence of friends and loved ones, and bring me to the understanding of Your everpresent friendship and love for me. In Your name I pray. Amen.

C. L.

Made for Each Other   2 Cor. 1:3–7

I'll never forget the day I met Nathan. I was taking the bus to Minneapolis; so was he. I had seen him in high school, but had never really talked to him. On the bus we shared a lot about ourselves, learned that we had many of the same interests, and vowed to keep in touch at college. Eventually we became close friends, and our lives have become richer through knowing each other.

Actually, we needed each other. Nathan told me about the day before the bus ride. He had stared outside at the rain dripping off the porch swing. He had wondered what he'd do when school started. How could he stand another year of loneliness and ridicule? He had dreaded being odd-man-out all over again, wondering when it would end. All the kids seemed to fit in except him. He always tried to be friendly, but the other kids would practically run the other way. He kept asking himself why.

I had felt much the same way. I'll never forget the emptiness, the ache of loneliness. I used to sit in my room for hours, reading and writing. I remember reading something from the Bible about Jesus suffering and dying so that people could be comforted. But at the time I wasn't. Still, I did feel some peace knowing that God would take care of my loneliness.

Then I met Nathan and understood. God had prepared us to comfort each other.

Prayer: Lord of all, comforter of the lonely, encourage and lift me up with Your love that I might be a comfort to others who are lonely. In hope, I pray. Amen.

D. V.

Nitai

John 14:18

Hurrying up the orphanage steps, the missionary tripped over a cardboard box. He started to kick it out of the way, but looked inside instead.

A baby just a few weeks old looked back with deep, dark eyes. His midnight-black hair shone like pure silk. A hastily scribbled note said his name was Nitai and that he needed a home.

There was no rosy future for this child. In a land where half of the children with both home and parents die of disease or starvation before their 6th birthday, what hope could there possibly have been for Nitai?

Two months later the answer came. A couple from America wanted to adopt him. He was no longer an orphan. Nitai would soon be held in his new parents' arms for the first time.

The love they gave him was given back. On his 10th birthday Nitai wrote this note to his parents: "Mom and Dad, you've made my life special. You chose me to be your child. You gave me love and life. I love you. Your son, Nitai."

What a beautiful picture of the love and life we've been given as the adopted children of Jesus Christ. We were orphans—separated from our heavenly Father by sin. But Christ's promise stands: "I will not leave you as orphans; I will come to you." In Christ, we have a place in God's family and a home with Him forever.

Prayer: Dear Lord, You have made my life special as You have made me Your child, a member of Your family. Your love is my comfort and promise. In the name of my Brother, Jesus. Amen.

D. V.

Going On

Staring into the empty soda can, Russ thought, "Why do my parents always fight? There must be some answer." His thoughts trailed off, and he lost himself in the unending pattern of his finger circling around the top of the can.

The phone ringing jolted him. "Hi, Lisa! How are ya?"

"Fine. Listen Russ, I've got a date with someone else."

Click. Dial tone. No time for explanations.

He angrily threw the can against the wall, grabbed the keys from his dresser, and flew out to his car. Tires squealing, he peeled out of the driveway and headed for anywhere, nowhere, across the railroad tracks, past the cemetery. Faster, faster—too fast—out on the stretch beyond the mall. "Who cares? Mom? Dad? Lisa?"

"Casting all your care . . . " A Bible verse, of all things, popped into his head. "Give me a break!" He slammed on the brakes, spinning the car in some gravel, and started to cry.

Through tears he could make out an enormous Vacation Bible School billboard. On it Jesus held out His arms, as if to Russ himself, and under that picture, Russ fell asleep.

"Son, son! You okay?" said a voice outside the car. Russ looked up, feeling awful. It was morning. Jesus was still there. And so was Russ.

Prayer: Lord, help me see Your love more fully, even when it seems invisible. Help me know how real Your promises are for me in every situation, no matter how terrible. You love me. That's something to hang on to. Amen.

D. V.

In a Rose Garden   Is. 58:11

"Lord, I'm scared. High school has been tough, and I'm not sure where I'm headed. I've been thinking—what am I going to do? What if I'm a total failure and my life is a complete waste? I mean, what have I got in my life that's going to bring success?"

Doubt grabs everyone at some point in life. It's frightening to be out of school with the real world looking you in the eye. Choosing a career is scary enough, but the responsibility of being on your own only seems to magnify the fear.

"Lord, I took a walk in a rose garden today. It seemed like the weeds had taken over. Some of the flowers were dying, and when I reached in to pick off the dead petals, thorns pierced my fingers. It reminded me of my life, Lord. When things get to me, I get angry with myself."

Maybe we're all like dying roses when our lives seem to be going nowhere. Others try to help us, but we put up walls of misunderstanding and hurt them like a thorn hurts the flesh.

"Lord, those flowers were beautiful, despite the thorns. They looked so strong and bright climbing the trellis. Maybe it's the rain You sent that brought life back again."

The support given to the roses climbing the trellis is a lot like God's love and concern for us. His Spirit is always available to guide and support us, and His grace makes life new again, begun in the water of our baptism.

Prayer: Lord, for rose gardens and rain, for renewal and hope, I thank You. I live confident of Your care. For Jesus' sake. Amen.

D. V.

Caught by Man

Is. 58:6

As the sun rises on her home in the small town of Lobabi, Tika is already putting on her work clothes. For 14 hours she won't see her parents, because they work in livestock barns miles away. Tika's job is to carry water to the field-workers. In one more year, this 9-year-old girl will be working the fields too. Tika is a victim of South Africa's policy of racial discrimination, apartheid.

Why are some people caught in a system that divides them by race or creed? It shouldn't be that way. Christ came to set us free from sin. God sent His Son to unite us with Him and with each other. But sinful people continue to weave webs of selfishness that trap others and oppress them.

What can we do, right where we are, for people like Tika? Prayer is most important. God's power works through the prayers of His people to change our world. And since God's Good News does change hearts, we can proclaim the mercy He demonstrated in Jesus Christ and the justice He desires. We can speak up for those who, like Tika, are still caught by man but set free in Jesus Christ.

Prayer: Lord, thank You for our freedom from the slavery of sin. Free our brothers and sisters throughout all the world, those who are caught by the sin of man. For Jesus' sake, use the power of Your Gospel to change the hearts of those who cause oppression. In Your name I pray. Amen.

T. J. H.

Prom Night Promise 1 Cor. 6:18–20

It's that one special night of high school, prom night. For some it's the biggest experience of their teenage years. It's also the night on which more girls get pregnant than in six months of Friday nights combined.

Tonight Chad and Julie will enjoy dinner, dancing, and a feeling of being grown-up. But the highlight of their evening will not be wrestling in the back seat of Chad's car, or making it on the beach, or being at some party where the kids are so high they don't even remember who they came with. Julie and Chad will spend the evening walking along the beach, not rolling in the sand; taking a moonlit drive, not driving the upholstery. As Christians they will honor God's expectations for them.

God tells us not to abuse our bodies sexually. Our bodies belong to God, not to us, because He made them and redeemed them with the blood of His Son, Jesus.

Back seat promiscuity is not God's idea of a great date. This doesn't mean Christian teens spend every date playing checkers and telling knock-knock jokes. Still we want to honor God and live as He wills. And He promises us the power to do just that.

More important we have His promise of forgiveness when we fall. He goes with us on the first date, to prom night, to the altar, and beyond.

Prayer: Lord, help me to stay away from sin and sinful situations. Give me strength to choose friends and dates that will help me to honor You with my body. Thanks for Your promises! Amen.

T. J. H.

I Only Love You Friday to Sunday

Ex. 20:12

"Time to go to Dad's house," Jim's mom yelled. That familiar phrase was yelled every Friday at four o'clock on the dot.

"Oh, goody," Jim thought, "another weekend at Dad's place. Nobody else around, no TV, and no hope of hearing music other than '60s garbage—just because some judge thought it would be good if I'd spend time with both caring parents."

Jim started down the stairs toward the kitchen. "Where'd you put those car keys, Mom?"

"They're already in the car. See you later, Hon. Love you!"

On the way to the car, Jim thought, "Does Mom really love me? Why have things been so tough between us? But, hey, Dad gives me $25 plus gas money for the weekend, no curfew, and even some beer. I can live with it. Off to another weekend of putting up with Dad and living for the night."

Jim's love for his parents has been strained by their divorce. He knows that God's command to honor parents goes for all children. Even in their hurt and loneliness, children of divorce can know the power of God's love. That love forgives us, and helps all of us to honor, love, *and forgive* our parents just as God loves and forgives all of us. He still works miracles today— even healing broken hearts and broken families.

Prayer: Lord, we know that in times of family trouble You act as Father to all. Bless all parents and children with Your strength to love, honor, and forgive each other. In Your powerful name. Amen.

T. J. H.

You Took Me In

It was 7:15 a.m. The only thought on the Alders' mind was the precious, smiling little girl they were about to adopt.

On the way to sign the final papers, Mr. Alders recalled a verse from the day's devotions: "In love he predestined us to be adopted as his sons through Jesus Christ, in accordance with his pleasure and will—"

We are those children. Christ loved us so much that He adopted us all to be His children and to have a home with Him. Following His example we want to do the same for others, sharing the same unselfish love.

Adopting a child is pleasing to God, but it also brings many joys to families. The effect upon the entire family, including natural children, can be awe-inspiring—especially when the adopted child is no infant. The joy of being accepted permanently, ending the eternal shuffling between foster homes, is a very powerful witness to the other children. We all need to appreciate the place we call home.

To be adopted feels good. When it happens we know we are finally welcome, wanted members of a loving family.

Prayer: Lord, Your love moved You to accept us as Your own. Help us share Your love with others so that they too might be adopted into Your family—and perhaps into our families as well. Amen.

T. J. H.

On Governments and Grasshoppers

Is. 40:21–28

Sue is a great sister alright, but she never met a cause she didn't like. She treats causes like lost puppies; she always brings them home. Now she's home from college, and posters flying every cause from saving Afghanistan to saving zebras cover her bedroom walls. Doesn't matter whether it's whale, seal, tree, or unborn baby, Sue is out to save it.

She makes me feel so guilty! I only save stamps.

Oh, I care for people and issues as much as Sue does, but I don't see what I can do (or Sue either, for that matter). Government is so big, and I'm so small that I told Sue I'd have as much impact as an insect. Do you know what she said?

"Nations and governments look like insects to God, silly. But God sees you as His child."

I'm no Sue, but I too have some deep concerns about war and peace, hunger and poverty. And I now realize my size in the affairs of state doesn't matter. I'm a baptized child of God. That means my brother, Jesus, is the King of kings. And I can talk to Him any time, about any issue!

Prayer: Dear King Jesus, thanks for the door open to Your throne of grace. I can sit by You and explain my concerns for this world of people You love. I pray now as Your little brother. Amen.

D. v.d.L.

Me? Wonderfully Made? Ps. 139:14

Who says that I'm fearfully and wonderfully made?

Oh, I know my body works okay. My fingers move when I want them to, and my feet go in the direction I point. Nobody who looks at me thinks I'm anything but a normal kid.

But what if my body isn't changing fast enough into that of an adult? Ever hear those laughs in the locker room, or see the sly smirks in the shower? Ever notice how no one respects you if you look younger than you are?

Ever have to sit through those health classes where the teacher pulls down charts of the human body and says, "Everyone matures at different rates"? What? Is that supposed to make me feel better when Sara turns me down for Dan because she'd rather go out "with a man than a boy"?

It's hard to praise You for my body, Father, when everybody else mocks it. And harder to thank You when I feel so shut out. I would think You'd understand that!

You do? Is that what the Bible means when it says Jesus "had no beauty . . . to attract us to Him, nothing in His appearance that we should desire Him" (Is. 53:2)?

But He sure was a man, Father—man enough to go to the cross! And, come to think of it, He did that for me.

Prayer: I've been unhappy with what I see in the mirror, Father. But I've been looking at me all wrong. You see a Christ-bought man, Christ's man. And You love what You see. Maybe I just needed to hear You tell me that again. Amen.

D. v.d.L.

no one will miss me

STOP!

who is it? don't bother me. i'm busy.

YES, I KNOW. IT'S I, YOUR GOD AND FATHER. SO STOP. NOW!

why? i have no reason to live. i'm going through with it.

NO REASON TO LIVE? WHAT DO YOU MEAN? TELL ME.

well, my friends don't think that i have any sort of brain inside my head; my parents don't listen to me; and, well, i'm just very sick of all the snobs at school teasing me.

I LOVE YOU.

stop it! don't say that. i'm not worth it.

WHO SAYS THAT?

everyone. i'm nothing but a nerd—to everyone and myself.

NOT TO ME. YOU'RE SPECIAL TO ME. AND I LOVE YOU DEARLY.

oh, yeah? since when?

SINCE BEFORE YOU WERE BORN. WHY ELSE WOULD I HAVE GIVEN UP MY SON?

okay, but why tell me this now?

BUT I'VE TOLD YOU MANY TIMES ALREADY—IN MY WORD. SOME PEOPLE DON'T UNDERSTAND THAT I LOVE THEM—NO MATTER WHAT. I WANT YOU TO LIVE, TO ENJOY MY ETERNAL LOVE, AND TO HELP ME SHARE IT.

okay, Father. I understand. what do I do now?

Prayer: Dear Lord, seems like I can't cope with this world and its demands on me. I feel like I can't go on living. I'm not quite sure I want to die, but I don't know if I can take it here anymore. Help me to cope. Amen.

K. W.

106

Victory over It   Matt. 4:1–11

It's the big moment. Your graded paper is put down in front of you, and you gasp with relief. You made an A! Sometimes all the studying and preparing pay off. You passed the test that was worrying you, thanks to God's grace and your work.

Yes, God's grace. Without it we'd be sunk.

In the Scripture reading, Jesus was tested by the devil. It was a different kind of testing, to be sure. Satan tried to convince Christ that all He ever wanted was within reach—if only Jesus would do what Satan asked.

Yet Jesus was not swayed. He knew that the devil didn't say what he meant, and He wasn't fooled by the devil's trickery.

Even today the devil is at work. He still tries to fool us. He asks so innocently, "Do you really need to study for that test?"

But Christ is there to help us. He fights off the devil for us and puts us gently back on the right track.

Whether it's a test or a temptation, whether it's easy or hard, it's great to know that our Lord Jesus is there for us.

Prayer: Dear Lord, when I am being tested, help me remember that You are with me. Remind me to call on You all the time. Amen.

K. W.

It Was a Lemon

In today's world many families are split apart by divorce. Children are shuttled between mom's place and dad's place, always living with tension and hard feelings. I know. I've been one of those kids for a long time.

I never thought it was much fun taking a trip across town to see my dad every other weekend. It never seemed right to have to leave my house to see him. We had been such a happy family. Why did my folks have to break it up and ruin my life?

It took me many years to realize that, in some ways, life is better now. Before they separated, I never heard or saw their love dying, their lives drifting apart. It wasn't until recently that I heard about all the problems they had hidden from me because they thought I probably wouldn't understand. That's when I realized how much they went through during the divorce. I wasn't the only one who suffered. My parents did too.

Understanding their struggles helped me look at them in a different light. They are real people, not just parents. They needed support through this as much as I did.

The healing that comes by forgiving and being forgiven has made us happier in the end. Sure it takes time for that to happen. But with God we've got time on our side.

Prayer: Dear Lord, help me to be understanding of my parents and to tell them how much they are loved, no matter what they've done or I've said before. Amen.

K. W.

Where Did I Go Wrong?

Ps. 31:9–16

Sondra doesn't want me around, I can tell. Lately, it seems like she and Laura have been doing all the things she and I used to do. People keep asking me if Sondra and I are fighting, and I don't know what to say. Maybe Sondra just got tired of me as a best friend and dumped me for Laura.

Sure, I was angry at first. Who wouldn't be? I was left!

Then I got to thinking, What good is being angry doing me? It's only making me bitter.

I realized there was only one course of action to take. I asked God to help me contain my anger and treat Sondra as if she were still my friend. Although I felt like no amount of praying could ever cover my hurt, I surprised myself by speaking to her in the hall the next day!

Through that experience, I learned that I can go to God when I need self-control. He puts everything in the proper perspective, and somehow I survive. Sondra's my friend again. And though it may never be exactly the same as it was, if it weren't for God I'd be a lonelier girl. When things get bad, I remember Christ on Maundy Thursday and the way His friends treated Him. Then I realize again how blessed I am.

Prayer: Dear Lord, I know that even if my friends leave me, in You I have comfort and hope. I pray that You will keep reminding me that You are there for me. Help me forgive my friends when they hurt me, and lift me up when I fall. Amen.

K. W.

Sunday Sleeper

Acts 20:7–12

"The reading for today is from the book of Acts."

Boy, I'm tired.

"Paul spoke to the people . . . until midnight."

Until midnight?! I hope Pastor isn't planning to preach that long.

"There were many lamps in the upstairs room where we were meeting."

Sounds like this church. Too bright. Too hot.

"Seated in a window was a young man named Eutychus, who was sinking into a deep sleep as Paul talked on and on."

Hey, I can relate to this guy!

"When he was sound asleep, he fell to the ground from the third story and was picked up dead. Paul went down, threw himself on the young man and put his arms around him. Don't be alarmed, he said. He's alive! . . . The people took the young man home. . . . greatly comforted."

Hey! I think I get the point. It's simple. That's what Pastor has been talking about this whole time. I guess I kinda let my mind wander. Now that I think about it, the Gospel message *is* pretty simple. Christ can touch us through others and make us alive.

Prayer: Dear Lord, I am human, but You know that. Sometimes my attention span isn't very long. For this reason I thank You for the Gospel message, which still cuts through my sleepiness. Amen.

C. B.

Soaking Up the Rays Ps. 4:6–8

Several sea gulls circled the pier as the morning surf struck the beach. I watched them closely as I crossed the sand, making my way through the maze of beach towels. Today was tanning day. It was a holiday and my first chance in a long time to get some sun. I had come fully prepared: tanning oil—the deep, dark, expensive kind—and my faithful portable stereo. I quickly set up camp and collapsed beneath the warmth from above.

I lay there for quite a while. The arm of the sea with its rippling muscles reached up the sandy slope to the spot where I lay, but it could not touch me. The sun, on the other hand, was far more successful. It took hold of me and warmed me— even the sandy spaces between my toes.

My eyes were tightly closed to the brightness, but this did not keep me from taking in the scene. I listened to the gulls and the children building sand castles; I smelled the wet sand and the salt of the sea.

I felt like I was in the palm of God's hand. After all, He made the sea and the sand. He also gave us senses to see, smell, hear, taste, and feel those things. He set the sun in the sky to give us warmth and to shed light throughout the world. So when I soak up the sun's rays, I'm soaking up a part of God's creation.

Prayer: Dear Lord, You called this world good, and I think I understand why. Thank You for the world You have made and the senses You gave me to enjoy it. Amen.

C. B.

His Name in Lights Ps. 19:1–4

My life often leads me through a black forest. I grope along in the darkness and stumble on the broken dreams that lie strewn across the path. No bird sings, no greenery grows. I wonder, if God is real, why does darkness permeate this forest?

Then I happen upon a clearing. I look up, and there is light. I see the stars . . . and then I remember: In the stars God's signature is reflected.

In the Old Testament God often announced Himself. He did things to show that He was there. Today, too many people think God is dead. They see no visions, they hear no voices from heaven, and they experience no miracles.

Ah—but maybe we're missing them!

In fact, while we are groping for God in the dark, He touches us. The rain watering the earth, the exam we aced when we expected failure, the friendly smile someone gives us in the hallway are all evidences that God is there.

He is in control. I have His word on that. I look at the stars and I remember: His name is there in lights.

Prayer: Dear Lord Jesus, Light of the world, the darkness around me sometimes makes me blind. But You came and spoke Your Word to me, telling me that while I was groping, You already had hold of me. Praise to You for created light. Praise to You for the uncreated Light of Your strong Word! Amen.

C. B.

The Pitter-Patter of Little Feet

Matt. 18:4

From my position in front of the bathroom mirror I heard the doorbell ring, and then the voices of my brother and his small family. I heard the usual ohs and ahs of my mom and dad as they laid eyes on their 18-month-old grandson. I smiled as I heard the baby sermonize in his own babbling.

I continued to comb my hair, pushing it back and forth, totally dissatisfied with the reflection I saw. My hair wasn't right, and neither were my clothes.

It wasn't long before I heard something coming up the stairs. I laid down the comb and turned to see what. I smiled again as my nephew popped into view above the top step. Somehow he had escaped during a diaper-change and was now dressed in nothing but his baggy Pampers. He was happy, and he didn't care a bit what he looked like.

Suddenly, from out of nowhere, my brother's fatherly hands reached out and took him. I could hear child's laughter as he was carried back down the stairs. He was totally satisfied.

I looked down at the comb on the counter and realized that I had just learned something from an 18-month-old.

Prayer: Dear Lord, help me to become like a little child. It seems that the older I get, the more concerned I become about unimportant things. Take me into Your Fatherly hands and help me to be content with what I am. Amen.

C. B.

I'm Called to Belong to You, Lord

John 15:12–17

I walk reluctantly along a busy airport corridor, a friend at my side. She loves with a big heart and a rare tenderness. We have grown very close during the writer's workshop, but now it's over. We have to say good-bye. Together we walk toward Gate 60, each step weighted by a feeling of emptiness. I am losing someone special. With every second we are closer to farewells and saddened hearts.

In this girl I find a deeper Christian love than I have ever felt before. It is a trusting love, a caring love, a love special to me because she shares the love of Christ. She helps me understand Jesus' great heart. He is a friend to everyone. He doesn't pick favorites. He cares even more than my friend does. And she *really* cares.

We enter Gate 60. It's time to go. I try to hold back the tears. Christy walks to her plane. I head on toward my gate. The reluctance is gone, replaced by grief and sadness.

Every human friend of ours will have to say good-bye sometime, but our Lord Jesus Christ will never leave us or forsake us. That is what makes Jesus' love so special.

Prayer: Dear Lord, I thank You for a love so strong that You will never leave us and for a heart so big that You will always love us. Many times I struggle with friends and friendship. In an ever-changing world, You never change. Thank You for Your presence. Amen.

L. R.

Fear Hides My Crying   Matt. 19:14

Tears pour from the terror-filled eyes of the young girl. She has been beaten for no apparent reason. Each blow from her mother has left a red imprint and burning sensation somewhere on her body. But the physical pain is nothing compared to the pain in the young girl's heart.

For Maria, this is a daily occurrence. Retreating to her closet, sitting among her stuffed animals, she sobs, hoping not to be discovered by her mom. This precious child does not understand what is going on, so she talks it over with her stuffed penguin.

Time passes and Maria falls asleep. She hears Jesus say, "The kingdom of heaven belongs to children. I love little children. I bless and care for you and all children everywhere. I was once a human child. I felt what you feel—pains of the body and of the heart. Whether you are verbally abused, physically abused, or mentally abused, you can turn to Me for comfort. I am your Rock, your Fortress, your Shield. In Me you can take refuge."

When Maria awakened from her dream she prayed:

Dear Jesus, please stay close to me. Please help my mom be happier so she stops hitting me. And help me love her even when she does. Please, Jesus, help our family live a better life. Amen.

L. R.

Victory in Death?   1 Cor. 15:54–57

The doorbell rang one cold winter evening. A soft-spoken uniformed police officer inquired, "Are you Mr. Christopher Simmons?"

Chris answered just as softly, "I am."

"I have some bad news. Your wife and mother were caught in the ice storm. Their car skidded off the road into the river. Both of them drowned." Mission completed, the police officer left.

Chris felt the trusting hand of his seven-year-old son Joshua slip quietly through his. How would Chris tell him that his mother and grandmother were dead?

Drawing in his breath, Chris explained death to Joshua in a way that he could understand. Chris' own words brought comfort to him as he spoke his faith aloud.

"Joshua," Chris said. "We can trust that God took Mom and Grandma to heaven."

Noticing a tear slip down his son's cheek Chris reassured him, "Joshua, it's all right to be sad. When Jesus' friend died, Jesus was sad and He cried. But Mom is not sad and neither is Grandma. It's hard to understand why someone you love dies. It's hard to understand how we win through dying, but we do. We win a victory through Jesus and live forever with Him. Mom and Grandma are alive with Jesus in heaven."

Prayer: Dear Lord, why do our loved ones have to die? Do You make it happen—or just allow it? At least You comfort me through our Lord, Jesus Christ, who gives victory in death. Amen.

L. R.

117

Daring Death   John 10:7–11

Christmas Eve, one year ago today, Jeff killed himself. He took his car, headed to Mount Mansfield, drove over the edge of its winding highway, and plunged 5,000 feet to the bottom of a rocky canyon. I sit at the foot of my best friend's grave and wonder why I didn't know.

As I think back, there were no warning signs. How could I tell that Jeff was really going to kill himself? Could I have stopped him?

I did know that he was not a Christian. I sit and wonder if I should have told him about the Shepherd who lays down his life for the sheep, or the one true God who shows us the right way along the path of life. Jeff might be alive if I had.

If I had told him, "Get to know Jesus, and follow in His footsteps. Turn to God for help. Let's pray together. Jesus died so you won't have to," maybe . . .

But Jeff hadn't wanted my help. I realize as I watch the falling snow gathering on his grave that there are certain times and situations in life that I cannot control. I have to trust God and remember that where He is, there is hope.

Praying softly, I speak these words to our Lord:

Jesus, a teenager's life is so full of awful surprises. There are many problems which we do not even recognize until it is too late. At least let us know that You are there to cast our cares upon, and that You love us even when we doubt ourselves. Amen.

L. R.

118

"I Like Sex!"   Gen. 1:27–31

Maybe you feel uncomfortable with those words. But God's Word tells us that He created male and female, as sexual beings, to be gifts for each other. And that is good!

The problem is that sex has been turned into something altogether different from what God intended it to be. Magazines, movies, television, and other media portray sex in negative ways. Sex is used to sell cars, deodorant, jeans, and beer. Sex has become a way to use and control people.

One problem these days is that too many people want to open these gifts at the wrong time. People are encouraged to give in to their sexual urges. Some people are so preoccupied with sex that it has become addictive—like doing drugs. Sex can hold tremendous power over us.

What do God's people do? First, we affirm sex as a gift from the Lord; we rejoice that He has made us male and female. We also affirm God's design—a monogamous relationship between one man and one woman for life. Then we can help each other talk through our questions, fears, concerns, and struggles. And we can go to our Lord when we mess up, giving thanks for His forgiveness.

Sex is a gift, a wonderful gift from God. I like sex!

Prayer: Lord, thanks for the gift of my sexuality. Help me to celebrate this gift and to use it wisely. When I fail in my relationships with others, reassure me with Your strong forgiveness and set me back on track. Thank You for making me as I am. Amen.

R. B.

AIDS Is a Four-Letter Word

Gal. 6:10

AIDS is no longer something to smirk about. It is so widespread that is causes us to reevaluate our own life-styles. It affects us all—young and old, black and white, male and female, Christian and non-Christian.

AIDS is the acronym for Acquired Immune Deficiency Syndrome. In our world, nation, community, social set, and family, AIDS has become an everyday word too.

Matt. 25:42–46 challenges God's people to help those in need—the hungry, the naked, the lonely, the hurting. It is relatively easy to provide food, clothing, and shelter; but when people have AIDS we quite naturally avoid contact with them for fear that we could be infected with the disease ourselves.

We must pray for the victims, direct and indirect, of the disease, for those filled with hate and prejudice toward the victims, and for ourselves as we learn about the disease so that we can reach out with compassion to the victims.

AIDS is a four-letter word. But we dare not let it blind us to the work that must be done.

Prayer: Lord, AIDS is a problem for me too. Help me see all people as You do, and show me how to love and care for them, for Jesus' sake. Amen.

R. B.

If You Love Jesus, Tell Your Face

Ps. 126:1–3

"Our mouths were filled with laughter, our tongues with songs of joy," writes the psalmist. If any people in this world have something to smile about, we do. We've been redeemed, forgiven, and loved into a joy-filled relationship with God.

This does not mean that God's people smile all the time. Life isn't that simple. We hurt. We mess things up. We forget about others. We become selfish and self-centered. And that makes our mouths droop and our smiles cease.

But rejoice again in the Lord. In Phil. 4:4–7, St. Paul reminds us that all of our rejoicing comes from the Lord. God, in Christ, is the reason for our joy. His Spirit leads us to the cross and empty tomb where we see what life is all about.

Look around you today. If you see people without smiles, give them one of yours in the Lord's name. And if today is not the best of days for you, catch a smile from other people whom the Lord has filled with His joy.

You have been touched by the power and forgiveness of the Lord Jesus! That's something to smile about!

Prayer: Giver of smiles, help me to see You in all that I do and say today. Help me to rejoice in You each day as You smile on me with Your love and forgiveness. Lord, let my life be a way and a smile by which You touch other people. In the name of Jesus, I smile. Amen.

R. B.

We Need Each Other! Rom. 5:10–11

Believe it or not, youth and adults need each other. Generation gaps and communication gaps notwithstanding, our Lord wants us, youth and adults, to minister to and with each other as we work, play, worship, and live together.

St. Paul explains the possibilities by pointing out that, because of sin, people become enemies of God and of each other. But Christ's death and resurrection bring people back together. People are reconciled to God and to each other under the cross and beside the empty tomb.

If the adults around you seem reluctant, then perhaps you will have to make the first step. Look for ways and places you can work together. Ask them to join you in worship and Bible study, on church committees and group outings. Perhaps you can start in your own home with your mom and dad. Sometimes we are surprised at how the Lord can work in and through each of us.

We need each other. We are friends together in the Lord. That's the way God planned it. It's a great plan—youth and adults together!

Prayer: Lord, thanks for bringing us together in Christ. Help me to see and love adults as fellow believers. And help adults see me the same way. Help us be friends in the name of our mutual friend Jesus. Amen.

R. B.

Scripture Index

Miscellaneous references within devotions and related passages are designated with parentheses.

Topical Index

FRIENDSHIPS

PRAISING GOD

PROBLEMS/TROUBLES

In General

Spiritual